THE MAN INSIDE

...THE **BLOODIEST** OUTBREAK

This edition published 2019

Big Sky Publishing Pty Ltd
PO Box 303, Newport, NSW 2106, Australia
Phone: 1300 364 611
Fax: (61 2) 9918 2396
Email: info@bigskypublishing.com.au
Web: www.bigskypublishing.com.au

Cover design and typesetting: Think Productions
Printed in China by Hang Tai Printing Company Limited

For Cataloguing-in-Publication entry see National Library of Australia.

Author: Graham Apthorpe

Title: The Man Inside: ...The Bloodiest Outbreak

ISBN: 978-1-922265-46-3

Front Cover Image: Courtesy of actor Yutaka Izumihara.
Back Cover Image: The view from the guard tower outside the perimeter of A Compound. AWM 064345.

THE MAN INSIDE

... THE BLOODIEST OUTBREAK

BIG SKY PUBLISHING
www.bigskypublishing.com.au

GRAHAM APTHORPE

This book is dedicated to the late Tony Ryan,
a good friend and a great reader.

CONTENTS

Preface to the Anniversary Edition 75 years after the Cowra Breakout ... vi
Foreword ... ix
Author's note ... 1
Introduction ... 4
Chapter 1 Japan at war ... 9
Chapter 2 Australia at war ... 20
Chapter 3 Just one Japanese soldier ... 28
Chapter 4 New Guinea ... 36
Chapter 5 Never be a prisoner ... 45
Chapter 6 Interrogate the enemy ... 53
Chapter 7 Naka's interrogation ... 66
Chapter 8 Build more camps ... 72
Chapter 9 Send him to Cowra ... 82
Chapter 10 Escape … to where? ... 89
Chapter 11 A matter of honour ... 102
Chapter 12 Court martial ... 108
Chapter 13 Other Cowras ... 120
Chapter 14 The descent ... 124
Chapter 15 Did we learn nothing from this? ... 135
Chapter 16 We choose to die! ... 145
Chapter 17 Home ... 160
Epilogue - a Judgement ... 169
Acknowledgements ... 177
Sources ... 179

PREFACE

TO THE ANNIVERSARY EDITION 75 YEARS AFTER THE COWRA BREAKOUT

In World War II, Australians and the Western Allies found the Japanese notion of death before dishonour to be a bizarre concept. For Japanese that dishonour with its origins in a corrupted version of Bushido, had its ultimate expression in the shame of being a prisoner. There were practical outcomes associated with this disgrace that would be heaped upon the family of the prisoner, such as social ostracism and even being cast out of their homes. Captivity was so alien to a Japanese soldier, sailor or airman that it rated not a mention in training or in any military manual. Suicide was the only option if the battle was lost and capture was likely. The uprising that became known as the Cowra Breakout resulting in the deaths of 234 Japanese was a fanatical and suicidal act and seemingly one to regain lost honour. It could have had no other outcome than huge casualties and that was precisely the reason for the Japanese leaders deciding on such an action.

The militant Japanese leaders found captivity unbearable, but what was more difficult for them was to inculcate their personal resentment into those ordinary soldiers under their command. These subordinates once removed from the battle, were enjoying relative comfort, medical treatment, safety and regular rations.

But there is a problem in taking the high ground when observing Japanese attitudes at that time, because for Australians, suicidal acts involving bravery are not so alien. In the revered folk song *Waltzing Matilda*, we hear "you'll never take me alive". Elsewhere the Bushranger Ned Kelly, in spite of his armour, was prepared for a hero's death. In the Great War of course, one of our most tragic moments was the 1915 charge at The Nek; just one of the follies of the Gallipoli campaign.

Bill Gammage wrote in his *The Broken Years* that when finished, the Australian dead were in an area the size of a tennis court.

So it is, that the notion of sacrifice has common ground across nations and culture, and if there was ever a bizarre coincidence, it is this: those Australians who died at The Nek almost to the day, just 29 years before, numbered 234. This was the same number of Japanese who died at Cowra.

Some may object to comparing Australian bravery to that of the Japanese in World War II, yet it was Australians, perhaps begrudgingly, who wrote and commented on it. Cowra POW Camp guard, Sergeant Wal Mackenzie, spoke openly about his time defending the northern gate at the Cowra Camp on the night of the Breakout. He was impressed by their bravery with rifle and machine gun fire directed at them, yet they did not falter up until the time they were hit. One who would become a prisoner of the Japanese and wrote of his experiences was Sergeant Kenneth Harrison, captured after the fall of Malaya and Singapore. He observed that the Japanese were fearless fighters, and that if there was to be another war, he would like his fellow Australians around him joined by "a Japanese battalion on my left and a Japanese battalion on my right."

The subject of this book is Lieutenant Maseo Naka. He could at least claim that his Japanese sense of honour was not entirely disgraced, knowing that rather than surrendering, he was captured, semi-comatose, sick and starving. Once recovered he recognised his guilt and like so many others who had not died in battle, could not attain a military death. With all the opportunities available, his few attempts at suicide were half-hearted, perhaps because they had no military significance. In Naka's case his taunting of the Australians at Cowra were his best efforts to restore honour to his lost soul.

Prior to the World War II years, Cowra was a town like so many others; rural, isolated and insular. It would transform in many ways and through the establishment of a Military training camp, a prisoner of war camp and various war industries, it would contribute to the war effort like no other town in Australia. It was however the blood sacrifice of the Breakout that would change it to become a place centred on peace and reconciliation. While many came on board, it was one man who would lead Cowra into a quite radical direction. He was Albert John Oliver MBE, but always called Ab.

Ab had served in WWII in the Middle East and later in New Guinea. He, along with other returned servicemen, took it upon themselves to care for the Japanese graves. This was barely a decade after the war and it was a precarious situation. There was no escaping the high level of post-war animosity between Australia and Japan, yet these men, led by Ab, maintained the simple, marked graves of the Japanese dead at Cowra.

Ab was a businessman and leader; unassuming but deliberate, and committed to his community. Among his many areas of community involvement were his 27 years as an elected local government official. He served as Deputy Mayor, Mayor and Shire President. In later life, Ab was asked his reasons for caring for the graves of a once hated enemy. He replied quite simply that when he was serving in the Middle East, he saw the WWI graves of the Australians and how well the locals had cared for them. His reasoning, and of those who helped him, was that while the Japanese had been an enemy, they were soldiers fighting for their country, and at least they deserved that recognition. "It was the right thing to do", he insisted. In addition to his MBE received in 1974, he would also be awarded in the same year, the Japanese Order of the Rising Sun. This prestigious award recognised his work for international goodwill and understanding and his contribution to the establishment of the Japanese Gardens and Cultural Centre at Cowra.

That simple act of regularly tending those graves at Cowra came to the notice of the Japanese Government and became the foundation for the very special relationship that Cowra has with Japan. That story and all that has come from it could fill a large volume, but for now that is sufficient.

Graham Apthorpe
Cowra

FOREWORD

Of all communities in Australia few were as affected by the Second World War as Cowra, a small service community in the central west of New South Wales. Until the war years Cowra was best known as a place on the way to somewhere else, with several major roads meeting the railway at the crossing of the Lachlan River.

In 1941 that railway disgorged Italian and from 1942 Japanese prisoners of war. Cowra became known as the site of a prison camp and then notorious as the scene of the war's largest prison-break. Other towns in Australia were affected by the war – Sydney had submarines in the harbour; Terowie saw Douglas MacArthur resolve to 'return'; Darwin was flattened by Japanese bombs; Thursday Island saw a greater proportion of men volunteer for military service than any other Australian community. But Cowra was the only place in Australia where civilians came face-to-face with their enemy, briefly at liberty among them during the notorious mass break-out in August 1944.

Graham Apthorpe, Cowra Shire's energetic Director of Corporate Services, has long been central to Cowra's efforts to recall and reflect on its heritage from the Second World War. He has been instrumental in highlighting Cowra's overall war effort in his book *A Town at War*. Cowra now remembers not just the camp and the events of August 1944, but has turned memories into a 'Festival of International Understanding'. Graham's present book, *The Man Inside*, itself embodies the idea of international understanding by revealing to us the life of Lieutenant Maseo Naka and his role in the dramatic events now at the heart of his town's history.

Graham's achievement in this book is that he reveals to Australian readers the life of one of the Cowra prisoners, who have overwhelmingly been unknown and often anonymous (partly because they concealed their identities out of shame at being captured). He has been able to do this firstly by making the most of the available Australian records (in

Maseo Naka's case because he was an unusually 'squeaky wheel' in the running of Cowra camp). But secondly Graham uses what we know of the life and death of Japanese soldiers in the Pacific war in general to reconstruct what we need to know about Maseo in particular. The Man Inside, it turns out, is not only Maseo Naka, but his fellow prisoners, fellow victims of the great conflict that made Australians and Japanese enemies and later, brought them together as friends.

The result, *The Man Inside*, is an illuminating contribution to the understanding of the war in the Pacific and to how – remarkably – the ideas, attitudes and character of soldiers of imperial Japan came to be indelibly associated with a community in rural New South Wales, not the last of the ties of blood between our two nations.

Prof. Peter Stanley
UNSW Canberra

AUTHOR'S NOTE

The Man Inside recounts the tragic story of Japanese soldier Maseo Naka.

In this account, I have tried to be as honest, direct and forthright as possible. I have attempted to acknowledge the many sources used but no doubt I have missed some and for these I apologise in advance. In addition to my own interest and research, I also recognise the tireless work of the many professional researchers and historians who have gone before me. I thank them sincerely and hope this story may add a little light and understanding to this tumultuous period of Australian and Japanese history. In dealing with the breakout event itself, I have drawn upon the research of the pre-eminent author in this field, the late Harry Gordon AM, coupled with the official documents of the day and from the various inquiries and court proceedings. I have over time been privileged to have spoken with both Japanese and Australians involved in this moment of history.

Japan's early victories gave its soldiers mythological status but with it came a reputation of utter and unrestrained barbarity which was not fully revealed until war's end. That trait became fixed in collective memory and has been a significant reason why Japanese soldiers, sailors and airmen have been seen as monsters. That they behaved monstrously in many cases is undeniable but if this is all we are prepared to consider, we have lost an opportunity to ask why it occurred. Maseo Naka, a junior officer, was a real person in a war that was none of his making and by all reports he did his duty with no hint of untoward actions other than those of a fighting soldier.

Why is he the focus of this book? It is simply because I saw him as a character leaping out of the drama that was the story of Japanese prisoners of war in Australia. Naka acted differently from the beginning; defiant and difficult, he tormented the Australians to the best of his ability. Unlike the others who had settled into relative complacency, he chose otherwise. While militancy from a small core of prisoners only emerged close to the time of the breakout, Naka's resolve was apparent from his first day to the end of his time there, leading to his very personal decline.

He was part of Japan, the seemingly unstoppable combative nation, confronting the Allies already frightened by the Great Depression and generally suspicious of Asia. Here was a world agitated, nervous and worried because of the Wall Street crash, with loss of hope and faith in governments and institutions. Naka was part of this Japanese warrior horde and for a short time his star shone brightly with the speedy victories in China, Pearl Harbor, Hong Kong, Malaya, Singapore, Philippines, Borneo, Netherlands East Indies and Rabaul. He was there as an infantryman and was buoyed along with success after success. But soon came the reverses. The USA was never going to let Japan forget its attack on Hawaii and brought its strong resolve to early military commitment, knowing that successes may not be immediate but that ultimately they would win. America 'cried havoc' and Coral Sea, Midway, Guadalcanal and island after island were victories. There was now a strong belief that this war could be won and Australia shared in these successes too: Milne Bay, Kokoda, Buna, Gona and Sanananda.

So it was that in New Guinea, Maseo Naka first sensed, and then met in battle, this growing and powerful force that was heading Japan's way. He was a player in this drama but his part was small, almost as an extra in a movie, appearing here and there in the acts and performances. He comes on stage and exits and returns at various times. The scene changes from a triumphant and victorious 'banzai' backdrop to one of banal and stark captivity and, in the desolation of imprisonment, he moves from merely extra to a leading role.

In this book, context is important and Japan's war is laid out in overview, as is Australia's experience and its response to Japan's entry. As well as a mighty military machine, here can be seen Australia and the USA's strong sense of humanity, expressed in treating a hated enemy with respect and often kindness. We spend time in meeting the history of the period and Naka's part in it, and we watch him move through this melodrama to the most tragic of outcomes in that Australian town of Cowra.

AUTHOR'S NOTES

This book's title, *The Man Inside*, specifically refers to Naka's time in Australia as a prisoner of war; 'Inside' also being one interpretation of his Japanese surname. 'Inside' also refers to the overwhelming sense of guilt and shame that so many Japanese prisoners of war internalised and which was one cause of the terrible events that unfolded in Cowra in 1944 in which Naka played a prophetic though indirect part.

Lastly, to all the Australian and Allied military personnel who contributed so much to defeat the Japanese Imperial forces in World War II … thank you.

INTRODUCTION

It was a few minutes before 7 am and the first glimmer of dawn was breaking over a cold, eerily silent winter's morning at the Prisoner of War Camp at Cowra. Senior officers and guards were still on alert at 'stand to' waiting, watching and no doubt replaying in their minds the terrifying events of the night. Officers' revolvers were now holstered but the guards' weapons were still held at waist level pointing towards B Compound where the quiet, still air was interrupted by the cries of the wounded and dying.

Most of these guards considered themselves tough old warriors, survivors from World War I, seasoned and not easily troubled. But in reality many were below par and not fit for active service as front-line troops. They had had no sleep the night before, they were exhausted and their tempers were frayed. Some had only returned from leave just before midnight.

But even for those who were hardened veterans of the carnage of Gallipoli, Palestine and Sinai, and the Western Front, the unfolding scene that the sun's rays slowly revealed was pitiless. The full impact of the attack which occurred some five hours previously stretched before them in all its brutal detail.

Each man, with barely a word spoken, looked on the masses of twisted, contorted bodies; congealed brown blood spilling into earthen drains; shredded flesh and brain matter macabrely displayed on the barbed wire. Now and then a tortured groan would rise from the few still alive. The dead who lay before them were just some of the 231 prisoners who would die in the uprising. Many of the 1104 Japanese armed with baseball bats, improvised knives, metal stakes and wooden clubs embedded with nails had thrown themselves at the barbed wire, machine-gun emplacements and guard towers.

In the orderly room behind the sentries lay the bodies of three Australian guards. These were Privates Ralph Jones and Ben Hardy, who had been clubbed and stabbed to death by the frenzied, suicidal waves of prisoners, and Private Charles Shepherd. Rumours had flown around that Private Shepherd had been accidentally shot by his fellow guards, but he was later found to have died at the hands of an escaping prisoner. One more Australian, Lieutenant Harry Doncaster, would die at dusk when ambushed on a patrol to find escaped Japanese.

The events of Saturday, 5 August 1944 during the early morning mass breakout of Japanese prisoners from the Cowra Prisoner of War Camp have been well documented in numerous historical and first-person accounts and it was in this breakout that Maseo Naka played a central, if indirect, role.

The coordinated, desperate breakout, part military operation, part mass suicide, exploded without warning at 1.50 am when a surging, screaming mass of Japanese prisoners charged in three well-organised groups towards the barbed wire internal perimeter of the camp. The first group headed east, attempting to break out of the camp towards Sydney Road; another ran north attacking the externally positioned Vickers machine-gun posts, overwhelming and killing the two guards manning the site and then attempting to turn the guns on the Australian lines. The third surged into the central access roadway area that bisected the camp's four quadrants that was colloquially known as 'Broadway'—the ironic name due to its 780-metre length of prominent lighting supposedly being reminiscent of New York's theatre district.

This third group split into two smaller units as planned, attacking the exterior access gates at both ends of Broadway. From there and over the fences, 300 prisoners ultimately escaped, spilling out towards the highway to Sydney and surrounding countryside. One was thought to have made it by train to Sydney but was found to be a Filipino sailor on leave! A handful of prisoners had made it over the wire in the face of withering and lethal cross-fire from the Vickers, but at a bloody cost. Their comrades had given their lives, under the code of personal sacrifice of the Japanese forces, to build a 'roadway of bodies' over which they ran, not to freedom, but in many cases into more bullets from the B Company sentries guarding the camp's exterior. Those who survived this second wave of fire sprinted through the night, escaping towards the Government Experimental Farm and the soil conservation stations north-west of the camp.

As well as the dead, a further three Australian guards had been wounded during the chaos and carnage by 'friendly fire' from other sentries. Of the hundreds of prisoners massing in Broadway, only one, a hut leader, escaped, subsequently killing guard Charles Shepherd with an improvised knife before being shot dead at close range. Despite the noise, fear and horror of the breakout, the whole bloody mess was over in around 20 minutes. Soldiers from the nearby Military Training Camp were there now in the deathly quiet and all were waiting for sunrise, unable to enter in the pre-dawn darkness, as all security lighting had been cut by a stray bullet.

The genesis of the breakout was in B Compound, the main Japanese prisoner complex within the camp. Standing outside the wire that morning was its commandant Major Robert Ramsay who, before his time there, had been awarded the Military Cross (MC) in the Middle East in 1916. He now observed the scene of slaughter with extremely mixed feelings. The attack had been quelled, but hundreds of fanatical Japanese prisoners had escaped into the surrounding countryside. There is no doubt that he was contemplating the future official inquiry where he would be called to detail the events leading up to that morning where he played such a pivotal part.

Guards later testified that many of the prisoners still inside the camp lay 'doggo' during the breakout for fear of being shot after apparently having second thoughts about the desirability of dying for their emperor. They may have had good reason to be scared; in the bloody chaos and brutality of the mass escape, some of the guards were accused of not having maintained military discipline. Complaints arose from fellow soldiers that Japanese prisoners, eager for an 'honourable' death, by standing up inside the camp demanding to be shot had been duly obliged. Medical records would also later show that there was at least one instance of a Japanese prisoner having been bayoneted in the back.

Despite the apparent surprise and confusion that the breakout caused the Australian guards, there had been a presentiment of the events of that night in 1943. Just 16 months before, Lieutenant Colonel Monty Brown, the Commandant of the No. 12 Prisoner of War and Internment Group, had pleaded with the military authorities to increase the security of the camp perimeters. Brown and commandant for the Italian C Compound, Major Edward Vivian Timms[1] held a number of serious conversations in Brown's office on the matter. They had also walked the perimeter wire together noting that the fences, barely six feet (1.8 metres) high, were no barrier to a determined escapee, let alone a mass of fanatical and determined Japanese prisoners.

This concern had arisen when a young Japanese officer, Maseo Naka, had clearly demonstrated the security shortcomings of the camp by escaping alone and with apparent ease. This singular event had provided a salutary warning that was well recognised at Cowra, but one that was ignored in Sydney, as decisions on prison camp security upgrades were often based on budgetary considerations.

In the end, and in spite of Brown's protestations, fence heights were not increased at the Cowra camp. On this bleak early August 1944 morning, the consequences of these indecisions now lay before Ramsay and his senior officers. That the young Japanese officer who had escaped in 1943 may not have participated in the breakout (as he was in detention in Sydney) was immaterial. While this officer had no involvement in the mass escape, his flight from Cowra, alone and unaided, had offered important clues that were ignored. As well as acting as an inspiration to his colleagues, his time at Cowra, his verbal outbursts and his altercations with authority revealed a deeply troubled and guilt-ridden soldier and provided an example of how Japanese prisoners might react as a result of their depth of shame. It also showed their ambivalent attitude to the Australians and that their soft treatment, often exceeding the provisions of the Geneva Convention, was viewed with contempt. Ironically, this relatively considerate conduct, partly because of the number of Australians being held prisoner by the Japanese, only added to their sense of shame. Most importantly, Maseo

1 Timms was an author and playwright who wrote the screenplay for Charles Chauvel's legendary movie *Forty Thousand Horsemen*.

Naka's evasion proved to his comrades that the security of the camp was severely compromised and escape was indeed a possibility. As will be shown later, Naka had also devised a clever way of informing the Japanese in B Compound about security arrangements. Now these same prisoners had proved it themselves and, although at a huge cost, 300 were now at large around the Cowra district.

Because of the strict martial and conformist nature of their beliefs and training, it was said that to understand one Japanese soldier was to know the group. Was the failure to understand one of these first officers captured and imprisoned in Australia, and who subsequently single-handedly broke out of the Cowra camp, to have drastic consequences for the events in 1944?

After what Allied intelligence had told the Australians about Japanese prisoners (including incidents at other camps overseas), and their strong sense of dishonour at being captives, why did the military authorities not design and put in place discipline and security procedures tailored specifically for them? As will be shown later, the Allies discovered that Japanese prisoners of war could, with careful handling, be controlled by various means and become compliant and reasonably passive, however those lessons were not put into practice when prisoners were put together in large groups. The wretched events of the breakout were ones where Lieutenant Maseo Naka played a central, if indirect, role. Did these deficiencies in understanding lead to not only the earlier escape of this one officer, but also to a significant intelligence and management failing, the Cowra breakout?

In essence, Maseo Naka's story, so familiar from the Pacific War, but in many other respects so unusual, proved to be a prelude to tragedy.

CHAPTER 1
JAPAN AT WAR

In the field of military history, the sheer scale, the moral dimensions and the bewildering brutality of World War II dominates. This enduring fascination has mainly concerned Nazi Germany and the war in Europe. The rise of the criminal madman Hitler and the inevitable road to war in 1939 has spellbound historians, both professional and amateur, with many thousands of books, documentaries and films written and made on the subject since 1945. Few, however, have shown the same interest in the fight against Imperial Japan and the war in Asia and the Pacific, almost equal in its magnitude, wanton cruelty, individual heroism and significance. This apparent lack of interest is probably as much to do with a dominant Western-centric view and general ignorance of this theatre of World War II as it is to do with our continuing fascination with the grotesque fascist regimes of Germany and Europe.

While relatively little has been told of the origins, cause and impacts of the Japanese war in Asia and the Pacific, even less is accessible on the background, motives and actions of the individual Japanese soldier and his experiences in that conflict. For many Australians, this lack of interest and knowledge may be understandable. There was a raw and genuine fear of an impending invasion after 1941. Combine this with the popular image of the Japanese soldier as an unthinking fanatic and the horrific treatment of Allied prisoners of war revealed in 1945 and there is, in many Australians of a certain generation, a strong sense of aversion.

There are still now a number of elderly men and women in this country who were civilian internees or prisoners of war and suffered starvation, brutality and worse under their Japanese captors. This unforgiving view of Japanese forces and individual soldiers is distilled in one of the iconic images of the war, a photograph found in the possessions of a dead Japanese soldier in 1944, showing Nippon cruelty in all its medieval theatre when dealing with Allied prisoners and civilians. The black-and-white photograph from New Guinea[2] shows captured Australian M Special Forces, Lieutenant Leonard Siffleet, kneeling bound, blindfolded and resigned to his fate, about to be beheaded by a sword-wielding Japanese officer. This form of execution of Allied prisoners and civilians by Japanese soldiers, even for minor or even symbolic infractions, was not uncommon during the war.

Australia's death toll in World War II has a particularly disturbing statistic, as fully 8,000 deaths from a total of 31,000 were as a result of Japanese maltreatment in their prisoner of war camps. Those 8,000 matched the 8,000 killed fighting the Japanese. Even then, these atrocities against Westerners pale into numerical insignificance compared to the millions of Asians who died of starvation, torture and summary execution and massacres during Japanese occupation.

The passing of the years has led to many Australians meeting individual Japanese and their families through trade, tourism and cultural exchanges. In business connections Japan quickly became a major postwar trading partner. To say that most Australians find the Japanese people to be charming, polite, engaging and welcoming is an understatement. Many Australians now have Japanese friends, sons- and daughters-in-law and grandchildren. How then does one reconcile these overwhelmingly positive personal experiences with the horrific events of World War II in Asia and the Pacific? How did a civilised cultural and economic success story with belief systems based on Buddhist and Confucian ideals of loyalty, family, and personal honour, descend into such barbarity mirroring the experience of Nazi Germany?

While not all Japanese were actively involved in Japan's aggressive militarism in the 1930s and 1940s, the truth is that these policies and their consequences enjoyed widespread and genuine support among the populace. In simple terms, Japan quickly became a feared military

2 Present-day Papua New Guinea was referred to as 'Papua' and as 'New Guinea' during WW2.

nation following the ending of the isolationist Tokugawa Shogunate between 1853 and 1867. Japan had no sophisticated forms of political dialogue, plurality of ideas, or means of representation and, like Germany, it came under a spell of mythical national glory based on military successes, which in turn drove economic imperatives. Once enchanted by this crude martial culture of conquest and exploitation, there were few remedies available to combat it. As a nation, Japan embraced a national cult based around racial superiority and emperor worship, ultimately drawing down upon itself almost total destruction.

The individual Japanese soldier's part in this tragedy is only now starting to be told. The intention here, however, is not to attempt a revisionist rewriting of history, trying to paint evil acts as less malign, but to instead offer through Maseo Naka's story a better informed and more rounded account of the ordinary soldier who performed, militarily at least, to an extremely high level. These mostly citizen soldiers, in reality, became brutalised captives at an early age within a martial system of obedience and racial superiority. They genuinely believed in the most part that their role was to serve and, if necessary, die for their country and their emperor. Even trivial orders from superiors were regarded as directions from their 'heavenly sovereign'. Conversely, if ever failing to carry orders out, regardless of the circumstances, it was better to die than to live. Added to this expectation was the threat of shame that would be heaped upon their family should they not do their duty. An extreme sense of honour was coupled with an indoctrinated hatred of Western society so it was little wonder that this created an almost perfect control mechanism to produce a fanatical fighting force.

It was only after cumulative military disasters from mid-1942, following the Battle of Midway and the defeat at Kokoda, that some of these men through their capture, isolation and exposure to Western Allies, saw that the myth of military invincibility was just that. From the millions in the Japanese military forces only a few thousand had an opportunity to rediscover who they really were. Some of these captives ended their war in various prisoner of war camps in Australia. Some stayed true to their beliefs to the end, to make amends and regain their lost 'spirit' by dying honourably in the largely futile breakout at the Cowra camp. One of these men came from the southern Japanese island of Kyushu and in his relatively brief military career caused considerable mayhem amongst his Australian captors.

The Man Inside is the story of one individual, Maseo Naka, and the events that involved him, from his enlistment, through to his final return to Japan after the war. It is an account that has been created using official records from this period along with other recognised documents and publications. While Naka's military story begins in Japan in 1940, its finale is with his capture in the bitter jungle-fighting between the Australians and the invading Japanese in New Guinea, battles that marked the end of Japan's military expansion. Because of the terrain and the desperate nature of the combat between these small groups of soldiers at close quarters, few prisoners were taken by either side. By December 1942, only 29 Japanese had been captured and by March 1943 when the Buna, Gona and Sananda campaigns were all but completed the figure of Japanese prisoners had risen to only 328. Up until the end of the war, even after three and a half years of almost constant fighting, Australia still had only around 4,000 Japanese prisoners with many of those held on behalf of the United States.

Maseo Naka's military career was relatively brief, but his fate, like millions of his fellow soldiers, was determined by the Japanese philosophy of 'spirit'. Commanders, junior officers, and individual soldiers all suffered from an almost mystical over-reliance on individual strength, determination and courage to win battles. This misplaced belief system became the flawed paradigm for Japanese military decision-making throughout World War II, to the ultimate detriment of ensuring efficient supplies, modern materiel and adaptable tactics. Ordinary soldiers, non-commissioned and commissioned officers, right up to commanders, were all subject to the same attitudinal deficiency which had inspired surprising, audacious victories early in the war, but which ultimately led to disaster.

This belief in the central importance of 'spirit' in individual soldiers had been moulded through societal and physical imperatives from an early age. Through rigorous training, physical hardship, and indoctrination, individual soldiers were taught to believe that 'spirit' (courage) rather than skill, resources or tactics was the vital ingredient that would bring him and Japan to ultimate victory. In spite of the limited technological advances made by the Japanese during the war (probably due in part to this belief) and a failure to adapt tactics despite repeated disasters, Japanese soldiers earned the admiration of the Allies for their courage and fortitude and were considered by many to be the best combat soldiers in the war. One Australian soldier with firsthand experience of the Japanese was Sergeant Kenneth Harrison who was captured in Malaya and held as a prisoner by the Japanese.[3] In a surprise admission, he described the Japanese soldiers in the following way: 'while they were appalling winners they were at least gracious losers' and 'One thing I know for certain; if there is another war and if I have to fight again, I would like my fellow Australians around me, and a Japanese battalion on my left and a Japanese battalion on my right.'

The Japanese infantryman, the sailor and the airman of the 1940s could not call upon a long tradition of designing, creating and using modern armaments, in direct contrast to the Western nations they opposed. Japan, however, had caught up quickly by carefully purchasing the technology of war from the West and applying modern military doctrine. Britain and Europe could draw on 1,000 years of military expeditions and experience and the United States and Australia benefited from these traditions as well as their own engagements. Through relentless and single-minded sacrifice and effort, Japan had emerged from a feudal society in the 1850s to develop an effective and expansionist military force in less than 90 years.

But while the modern Japanese soldiers appeared to be feared 20th-century warriors, they were philosophically trapped in the past with each individual taught to view themselves as an embodiment of the samurai code of Japan's ancient warrior class. In stark contrast, Western military tradition had long since discarded feudal notions of the life, death, honour and purpose of being a soldier. Consequently, their

---

3 Author of *The Brave Japanese,* 1966.

standing armies in peacetime were relatively small and only expanded exponentially in time of war or when under external threat. The men who had created the new Imperial Japanese Army, were the generation following the last of the samurai and while they adopted rifles and machine guns, warships and cannons, they did not completely abandon the old ways, but rather adapted them for a modern fighting force.

While their training created a fearless soldier, the warrior mentality often led to almost insane tactics where soldiers would attempt to gain proximity to the enemy so as to engage in hand-to-hand combat in the style of the samurai. Ancient traditions mixed with modern weaponry created a heroic, physically brave soldier, but who also had limited moral boundaries and little or no understanding of the rules of war. Here was a soldier who could move easily from extravagant chivalry to its absolute opposite: brutal inhumanity. Barbarities and atrocities in times of war are not uncommon and were not isolated to the Japanese during World War II. It has also been a recognised phenomenon in a number of theatres of war, that soldiers who are generally well behaved in their homeland feel far less confined to moral codes and social strictures when in combat on foreign shores. Even considering the extremes of World War II, Japanese soldiers were guilty of a wide range of atrocities including general maltreatment and killing through the neglect of prisoners and civilians, mass rape and enslavement. In the entire indoctrination process that led to these crimes, those who were controlling Japanese society used a range of psychological, emotional and cultural mechanisms to call upon each man, woman and child to recognise and obey the rules laid out before them.

After deciding to become a Western-style imperial power, Japan sent representatives to Europe to scrutinise modern military operations at close quarters. Having been previously impressed by the French and intent on learning more from them, they observed the outbreak of the Franco-Prussian war in 1870. Fascination with the French way quickly evaporated when the Japanese representatives saw that Paris had fallen to the Prussians, so they immediately changed their travel plans and headed to Berlin, the capital of Prussia. Upon their return to Japan, they recommended that Japan should adopt the 'Prussian system' with particular emphasis on the relationship between the military and the state. In spite of their fascination with Prussia, Japan still adopted French military systems at that time.

The year 1870 also saw the introduction of conscription for military service. Although it was not fully observed and was regularly evaded, it was considered more important to Japan to have a system in place rather than to have it actually operating! Progressively, Japan was adopting European military, economic and cultural systems, but still with one foot in the past. Modernisation and exposure to the West also introduced ideas of plurality, party politics and democratic principles, but with a resultant determination by the militarists that they would not relinquish the power they had held for the past 800 years. They would not be held accountable by the people through any democratic medium and instead instituted strong mechanisms of persuasion to control the Japanese people. The militarists did not have complete control of the public purse and confrontations occasionally occurred between them and the Japanese parliament (Diet) and one budget battle in 1892 saw the Diet dissolved. The emperor personally intervened with ¥300,000 from the Imperial Purse together with a requirement that government salaries be reduced by 10 per cent to fund further military expansion.

Victory for the Japanese military machine soon followed with a solid track record of successes ranging from the incursions into China in the 1890s, victory against Russia in 1905, the subsequent annexation of Korea and Formosa (Taiwan) and, finally, the lightning strikes on Pearl Harbor, Hong Kong, Malaya and the Philippines in December 1941. Japan had achieved all these successes with a newly modernised navy and air force based on the template of Western imperial powers, but, crucially, its infantry had retained the small arms typical of the late 19th century.

Japan's excursions in China and Manchuria in the late 19th century were essentially local wars, highlighting in the minds of its generals issues of resources and extended lines of supply for fighting armies. Manchuria could supply those much needed raw materials that Japan has traditionally lacked. Japan's militarists learned a great deal in

China as well as from their victory over Russia's far eastern territories in 1904–5. While not a combatant in World War I, Japan was an observer on the Western Front in France and Belgium. The sheer mass of men and armaments in these battles showed Japan the huge demands that a world war placed on materiel and natural resources.

During this period, Japan had also experienced the patronising way the West viewed Asia and Asians and also the perceived Japanese threat. The supposed European and American efforts to crimp and limit Japanese power and influence have been debated and speculated as being large contributing factors leading to war in 1941. For instance, in 1922 at the Washington Conference, the United States prevailed upon the five principal naval powers to agree to limits on naval strength for ships of the larger classes. Japan was at first unwilling to accept naval inferiority but reluctantly agreed, only when it was decided that the United States would not further develop any naval bases west of Hawaii, and Britain no bases further east of Singapore. These restrictions would initiate future tension and be of vital importance in World War II, but did not appear to be of immediate military importance at the time. Australia, though relatively naïve in world affairs had already recognised their potential effect. In the previous year in preparation for talks on naval disarmament, Australian Prime Minister William (Billy) Hughes made an important speech to parliament. A combative figure much loved by newspaper cartoonists, he had figured prominently at the Versailles Peace talks after World War I. Hughes noted that only 285 nautical miles separated the protectorates allotted to Japan as a result of their assisting the Allies in World War I and Australia's similar acquisitions of previously German-controlled New Guinea. Often disparaged as a warmonger, Hughes's concerns in 1921 would prove prophetic.

Hughes in this speech articulated the unease of not only Australia, but other interested nations, by declaring that the Pacific 'problem' was also a Japanese 'problem'. Japan had modernised quickly; had a growing population on a small, resource-poor island; was running short of these materials and also wanted expanded markets for its goods urgently. Hughes identified historically the result of this general problem for powerful nations. He said that countries so affected invariably ended up 'hacking their way to the fertile pastures of their neighbours'. 'Where were the Japanese people to go?' he asked. 'Not to Australia or the United States, but to China!'

At the beginning of the 20th century, Japanese militarists saw immense value in resurrecting parts of the lost samurai warrior tradition to aid in their control of society. They re-engineered traditional Zen and Confucianist beliefs into a propagandised system of martial traditions, with the aim of developing expansionist militaristic characteristics not only in the army, but in society as a whole. Central to this philosophy was allegiance to the emperor to the point that every action in one's life was seen as either 'honouring' or 'dishonouring' their living god. Emphasised also were the virtues of self-sacrifice and deprivation, faith, trust in officers and fellow soldiers, uprightness, thriftiness, valour and frugality. The important outcome of these qualities was a highly developed sense of shame at personal failure. As sudden death was not an unusual event for the ordinary citizen at this time in Japan's history, fear of it was not strong. Soldiers were constantly re-enforced with the belief that, in battle, they should fight to the death or, in defeat, kill themselves. A common mantra summarising this belief went: 'Duty is weightier than a mountain; death is lighter than a feather.'

The Japanese people were also conditioned, not only at a military level but also within civil society, to respect their elders, to obey authority figures in the workplace and to believe that the emperor was a deity. Australian priest Father Paul Glynn, a Marist missionary in Japan for many years, believed that the Japanese soldiers' psychological conditioning was greatly influenced by adherence to the Bushido code manipulated by the militarists of the 1930s and 1940s who used the same rallying call, the all-important virtue of the samurai dying willingly for his liege (lord). Japanese soldiers were, then, to become the new samurai of a new empire.

The Bushido code had become nothing more than a bastardised means of control. 'Bushido' is a word often misunderstood in Western society and was similarly misrepresented and exploited by the militarists in Japan. Legendary Japanese author Inazo Nitobe wrote his seminal book *Bushido: The Soul of Japan* in 1899 in an attempt to explore this unique way of life and its influence on Japanese society. He asked whether Western civilisation, in its inexorable march through Japanese society, had already wiped out every trace of this ancient discipline. Nitobe, who mixed freely with Westerners and thoroughly understood Western society, compared Bushido with traditional European codes of chivalry and as represented in the Victorian-era novel *Tom Brown's School Days*. Set at Rugby School in England in the mid-19th century, this work was hugely popular in Japan with its emphasis on the importance of physical development, boldness, fighting spirit, sociability, morality and idealism. Conversely, Bushido's appeal is in the power of deciding, without wavering, upon a certain course of conduct in accordance with reason and being prepared to '*die when it is right to die*, to *strike when to strike is right.*'

Bushido also requires its practitioners to understand that the feeling of distress is the root of benevolence because a benevolent man is always mindful of those who are suffering or in distress. Nitobe noted that, when taken too far, Bushido's emphasis on self-control and discipline can 'repress the *genial* current of the *soul*. It can *force pliant natures into distortions* and *monstrosities*. It *can beget bigotry*, and *breed hypocrisy.*' Nitobe said that, while death with honour was accepted in Bushido as an ultimate solution to intractable problems, the aim of the ambitious and successful samurai was to not let problems get to this state of affairs. It was, as Nitobe explained, 'a process where warriors could expiate their crimes and apologise for errors, escape disgrace, redeem their friends or prove their sincerity.' The performance of *hara kiri* or '*seppuku*', a ritual self-disembowelling with death subsequently assisted by another who would behead the suicidee, was to Oriental sensibilities the ultimate symbolic act, exposing as it did the pelvic and abdominal 'brain' to observe its nature.

Nitobe observed disdainfully that this type of suicide had simply become fashionable. 'For causes entirely incompatible with reason, or for reasons entirely undeserving of death. Hot headed youths rushed into it as insects into a fire; mixed and dubious motives drove more samurai to this deed than nuns into convent gates.'

Chinese philosopher Mencius, a second-century BCE interpreter of Confucius, wrote that:

> When heaven is about to confer a great responsibility on any man, it will exercise his mind with suffering, subject his sinews and bones to hard work, expose his body to hunger, put him to poverty, place obstacles in the paths of his deeds, so as to stimulate his mind, harden his nature, and improve wherever he is incompetent. ... To avoid what heaven has in store is an act of cowardice.

When explained and understood, there are many aspects within Bushido and the teachings of Confucius and Mencius that have a familiar appeal to Westerners. Nitobe was able to identify the positive aspects of Bushido and how it formed Japanese society. His genius was being able to set down and define the principles of Bushido for someone unfamiliar with Asian forms of philosophy and thought. Because of his work, it is easy to observe how its chivalrous notions were manipulated and re-engineered by the leaders of Japan's militaristic society into a part fascist, part Confucian compound. European chivalry was based in its purest form on a philosophy which has, as its essence, the living of one's life in a right and proper manner. The militarists in Japan, on the other hand, focused, in the most devious and deceitful way, their ideals of 'chivalry' and 'honour' on blind obedience and twisted notions of death before dishonour. In the most concrete and calculating way, the militarists in the 1930s and 1940s were able to control the Japanese people and its soldiers, leading the nation to its ultimate millions of deaths and a destroyed society.

Small bit player though he was, Lieutenant Maseo Naka was faithfully performing his role in a tragic drama, reading from an expurgated and corrupted Bushido script.

CHAPTER 2
AUSTRALIA AT WAR

Maseo Naka was about to collide with 1940s Australia, a very different place to what it is today. The postwar migrant boom; the expansion and enrichment of the middle classes with huge new suburbs on our cities' urban fringes; the explosion of popular culture with television, rock music, public protest and personal fulfilment; the advances in technology, medicine, living standards and life expectancy were all to come. Even as a young nation barely 150 years old, it had achieved much: a functioning and representative democracy; an independent judiciary; religious freedom; an unconstrained media and the foundations of a welfare system. There was also a reality about its youthfulness. As a culturally dependent European outpost of about seven million citizens, mostly of English, Irish, Scottish and Welsh heritage, it had much to learn about the world, international politics and mature relationships with its neighbours and allies.

At the outbreak of war with Germany in September 1939, Australia was still suffering the effects of the Great Depression, an economic collapse starting in 1929 that saw mass unemployment in most economies, deflation, social unrest, the rise of political extremism in many countries and declining world trade. It was a bleak and austere period in Australia (with one in four workers unemployed) which paradoxically brought out both the best and worst in its people.

Older Australians speaking about those years recall how families and relatives pulled together, the constant shortages of food and goods, how mothers would be forced to scrub floors to bring in a few shillings each week and sadly about how some people just gave up. At the time of the Wall Street crash in August 1929, Australia already had a 10 per cent unemployment rate and, as a trading nation of natural resources, was particularly hard hit. Therefore, while the effects of the

Great Depression took some time to take hold in the United States, it was felt almost immediately in Australia.

Going to the aid of the British Empire in World War I was considered a great patriotic duty, an adventure in which Australia could play its part but with little foresight regarding the likely human costs of the four-year conflict. Having to suffer the extreme privations and the severe economic drain on top of the huge casualties of a modern industrial-scale war was another issue altogether. The most significant effect of that war was that just over one man in five who had served overseas had been killed, around 60,000 men out of a nation of about five million. Almost as devastating, a similar number would die from their wounds, suicide, lungs ruined by gas, and other privations in the 20 years thereafter.

In 1929, Australia had sent a delegation to Britain to seek relief from its vestigial World War I hardships, principally those associated with debts to the 'Mother Country'. It was, realistically, viewed as a 'cap in hand' mission and unlikely to succeed. In August 1930, the Australian Labor Party's NSW Central Executive called upon the Federal Government to make representations to Britain on the number of significant economic sacrifices that Australia had made to help that World War I effort. Both appeals were unsuccessful.

Australia had huge debts from both the war itself and from the continuing costs of establishing one of the world's first welfare systems for injured and incapacitated ex-soldiers. Not only had it experienced a vast number of fatalities (60,284 in total), but there were also 155,000 wounded to care for. After the hospitalisations and care for returned soldiers stabilised in numbers in the early years after the war, they began to climb rapidly from 22,742 in 1926, to 35,550 in 1933 and 49,157 in 1939 at the start of World War II. The principal causes of the increases were for lung problems (from gassings), gunshot wounds, tuberculosis, and war neuroses (post-traumatic stress). For the young men who had suffered the industrial-scale slaughter at Gallipoli and on the Western Front, war had cast a long shadow indeed.[4]

4 The author's grandfather, wounded in 1916, died without warning in 1947 as a result of shell fragments having moved in his lungs.

The continuing and increasing cost of caring for these survivors of World War I compounded the devastating economic impact of the Great Depression on individuals and society. Many older Australians still have vivid memories of no work, limited food and clothing, and sustenance ('susso') for those on unemployment benefits ('the dole'). Austerity meant not wasting a morsel of food and saving every last penny, miserly habits which many retained even decades later. In those dire years, many lost their homes, unable to pay rent or keep up house repayments. Shanty townships sprang up on the edges of cities, comprising corrugated-iron shacks with poor sanitation that were prey to the extremes of weather. Winter and summer extremes increased rates of communicable diseases for which there were few effective treatments, especially tuberculosis (TB) which in those days was the feared fatal disease. The opportunity to grow your own food, keep poultry and catch rabbits for cheap protein meant that people in country areas probably fared better than their city counterparts.

As with Europe and the United States, there were serious and unsettling political consequences of the Depression as many Australians simply lost faith in government and politicians. In their desperation, many were attracted to radical parties on the political right and left. Fascist groups modelled on the European ideologies of Hitler and Mussolini grew as did the number and power of socialist and communist organisations. One theatrical instance of the appeal of these groups was the sabotage of the opening of the Sydney Harbour Bridge in 1932 by 'ribbon cutter' Francis De Groot who was masquerading as a NSW Mounted Policeman. His self-styled 'New Guard' was a semi-fascist paramilitary group comprising many disaffected World War I veterans opposed to NSW Labor Premier Jack Lang's social welfare program. Some of these men would later re-enlist as prisoner of war camp guards at places like Cowra and some would end up dealing with Japanese prisoners such as Maseo Naka.

While Pearl Harbor is generally and rightly viewed as a treacherous and unprovoked surprise attack on a neutral nation, it would be naïve and disingenuous to say that such an incident was totally unexpected. The strike against America's Pacific naval fleet by Japanese bombers and fighter planes on the morning of 7 December 1941 was not a complete surprise. Australia, Britain and the United States had long recognised the inevitability of Japan's newly found confidence, aggression and imperial ambitions manifesting itself in some form, sooner rather than later.

Until France fell to the Nazis, rapidly and surprisingly, in June 1940, Australia was prepared to take a back seat and let Britain and the United States use their diplomatic skills to ensure that Japan stayed out of the war. Australia was assured, at least officially, by the announcement of Japan's Prime Minister Nobuyuki Abe on 4 September 1939 which essentially stated that the Japanese people would not be involved in the European conflict but would concentrate on settling their long-running imperial war in China. Australia sought assurances from Britain that it was playing an active role in the discussions to keep Japan out of the war between the Axis and Allies and, as a result, was reassured and confident enough to send its troops and navy to the Middle East and the Mediterranean. In these theatres, the Australians were instrumental in assisting the defeat of the Italians and Germans in a number of battles—combat experience that would prove invaluable in the New Guinea campaigns despite the vastly different terrain. Australia was, nevertheless, keen to ensure that Britain did not 'aggravate' any situation that might provoke Japan to lash out. Japan's threatening rhetoric continued to escalate in June 1940 following the downfall of France with its announcement that, while it was constructing a 'new order in Asia', it was also paying serious attention to events in various quarters, including the 'South Seas' (South China Sea and the Pacific). Japan issued a statement that any change to the status of a number of South Pacific and East Asian locations would be 'of grave concern to its people'. As with the fascist powers in Europe, the Japanese were using the rhetoric of self-defence as a means of escalating an engineered crisis. While the meaning may have been somewhat obscure, it implied a serious threat, and one on which they were to immediately act. Japan quickly and officially joined the Axis powers and presented a series of demands to the United Kingdom. They were to withdraw their garrison in Shanghai and close the Hong Kong frontier and the Burma Road. From this point on, Australia's fears increased exponentially as it had every reason to believe that should Japan declare war, Australia would be the chief object of a Japanese attack.

Alarmed by these developments, the conservative Menzies Government quickly changed its language and forcefully expressed to Britain its strongly held view that it no longer supported a policy of 'mere appeasement'. The Australian Government's opinion was that, while Japan seemed intent on war, British diplomacy should be firm but, if possible, still avoid war. For the remainder of 1940 and 1941, the Australian Government supported the British and American economic sanctions against Japan which were designed to downgrade and limit Japan's military and overall industrial capacity.

These targeted measures had been instituted primarily because of Japan's military aggression and their war in China. The sanctions were intended to prevent Japan from accumulating the resources it would need to wage further aggressive expansionism or to transfer these resources to Germany and the other Axis powers. The trade war and war of words escalated and as a counter-measure to Japan's occupation of French Indochina (now the countries of Vietnam, Cambodia and Laos), one year earlier, Australia agreed with Britain and the United States to freeze Japanese assets and cease nearly all trade. While the agreement was confirmed by all sides, Australia was still concerned that Britain may lag in enacting provisions of the sanctions in concert with the United States so sent a telegram to that effect to Britain. This approach was typical of Australia during this tense pre-war period. As a geographically isolated junior player in this partnership, Australia regularly felt the necessity to plead its concerns before the British and Americans, sometimes imploringly and sometimes with desperate urgency.

Sanctions, however, began with Prime Minister Robert Menzies reporting to the Australian Advisory War Council that a 'chalk line' should now be drawn to limit Japan's advances in Asia and that the economic measures against Japan should be 'all embracing and crippling'. Menzies subsequently issued a further communication to the other Dominion prime ministers (Canada, South Africa, New Zealand), expressing the view that, in the event of Japanese retaliation because of these sanctions, the United States should 'resolutely advise' Japan that it would be prepared to go much further with these measures. Menzies believed that such a stance by the Americans might force Japan to reconsider its expansionist plans. It was quite clear that Australia at this time saw the United States as a bigger, better player in this game than the British.

Often unfairly portrayed as a slavish Anglophile, Menzies recognised that taking such a strategic position came with serious risks, but so did doing nothing. He theorised that, if the Australian, American and British positions were not communicated with nuance and balance, Japan could be forced into the situation where it could not withdraw without serious loss of 'face', which even then was understood as a potential serious strategic error that could have dire consequences.

During the lead-up to what now appeared to be an inevitable war with Japan, Australian diplomacy swung from going hard with an almost bravado approach, to withdrawing to a more considered position. On the one hand, Australia sought to put pressure on Britain and the United States to act strongly in dealing with Japan because of its long-held belief that, should Japan go to war, Australia would be its principal target. On the other hand, it also advised caution in these demands so as to not provoke Japan to go to war, with Australia again as a major target. In many ways it was a 'fence-sitting' exercise and Australia was good at it.

Because of our small population and geographical vulnerability, the Australian Government saw little room for independent, unilateral action in these matters. The Japanese were also playing games with their diplomats in Australia suggesting that Menzies could go to Tokyo. Mindful of British Prime Minister Neville Chamberlain's disastrous diplomatic missions to Germany and his discredited policy of appeasement, Menzies rejected the idea.

The fast-developing crisis led to many different scenarios in the minds of the Australians and their government concerning what Japan might do next and how the United States should address the situation.

In August 1940, the future of the independent kingdom of Thailand became a flashpoint with the Japanese stationing more than 35,000 troops in adjacent Indochina, with Thailand a tempting northern gateway to both British Malaya and Singapore. The Australians were again caught between two contradictory positions; Menzies informing the Australian Advisory War Council on 14 August 1940 that, if Japan attacked Thailand, Britain would go to war even without the United States, provided that the Americans did not object!

Frantic communications continued on the Japan issue until, finally, American President Franklin Roosevelt provided a diplomatic warning to Japan which was less forthright than both Britain and Australia had expected. Nevertheless, the warning did provide an unambiguous threat of retaliation by the United States against Japan in the eventuality of their further aggression. Britain subsequently stated that it would support the United States in opposing Japanese aggression and that it would issue its own communiqué to this effect. Australia's new, but only short-term Prime Minister Arthur (Artie) Fadden then received a telegram from British Prime Minister Winston Churchill referring to the situation in the 'Far East' as 'not only as more favourable but as less tense'. Churchill added complacently that, as they became available, Britain contemplated placing a force of naval ships in the Aden–Singapore–Simonstown triangle to Australia's north. At this point the Australian Government relaxed a little and thanked Churchill for his actions.

The Allies continued to speculate on the fast-moving international situation in Asia and focused their speculations on the possibility of Japan attacking Russia. The Soviet Union, formerly a German ally, had been invaded by the Nazis in June 1941. Completely unprepared and suffering huge casualties, it was immediately and disastrously on the back foot, so much so that it was considered a strong possibility by the Allies that Germany may defeat Russia by Christmas.

British intelligence on the supposed attack on the Soviet Russians by Japan proved delusional. Having consideration to its failure to predict the events in the Malay Peninsula a little later, it was also shown to be unreliable and patchy at best. The British estimation, either through wishful thinking or incompetence, was that Japan was concentrating its forces against the Russians in the north. Because of the restrictions of the tropical monsoon between November and February, any strike to the south was seen as highly improbable.

Fatally, Britain also felt at this time that Japan, suffering from the American and British trade embargo, was now susceptible to negotiation. We now know that the Allies were ultimately on a fool's errand with any of its attempts to negotiate peace with Japan. During this period the Japanese Government had committed at its Imperial Conference on 2 July 1941 to 'strike' against the West and although this decision had been overturned by the emperor in September, the decision to 'go' was again made on 1 December 1941. Commander-in-Chief Admiral Yamamoto's audacious plans had their genesis 14 years earlier and were finally approved. The Kido Butai ('mobile force') was on its way to Pearl Harbor.

Not only was America's Pacific Fleet at Hawaii attacked on 7 December, but also independent Thailand and British mandate Hong Kong. Lieutenant Maseo Naka had also now moved with his 41st Infantry Regiment from Indochina and was ready to attack Thailand. His destiny, decided anonymously in numberless war meetings, official communiqués and diplomatic negotiations, would take him all the way down the Malayan Peninsula to Singapore, to the Philippines, New Britain, Kokoda and finally to Cowra.

CHAPTER 3
JUST ONE JAPANESE SOLDIER

Maseo Naka as an officer in the Japanese Army was a product of his time, place and circumstances. As a soldier, he was moulded by that unique mix of Confucian respect for authority and obedience, the Bushido (literally 'the way of the warrior') code of honour of the samurai caste of feudal Japan, matched with the 1920s aggressive militarism of the fascist powers in Europe.

This singular alloy of personal submission, an unwavering sense of self-sacrifice and duty and collective aggression, was encapsulated in a US Army publication provided to American troops during World War II to help them understand this formidable enemy. Titled *Soldier's Guide to the Japanese Army*, it provided a thorough summary of a typical Japanese soldier's entry into the army, their training, uniforms and equipment, rations, weapons, organisational structure and tactics. All soldiers were encouraged to read these bulletins and publications which were provided throughout the war on a range of subjects.

The typical American soldier's understanding of Japanese society and people at that time was based on racist caricatures and stereotypes and popular legend. The purpose of these pamphlets and publications was, therefore, to inform and dispel the lack of information that provided fertile ground for myth-making and which, unless refuted, assumed the status of fact.

So how did the Japanese soldier become the brave, ruthless fanatic of contemporary newsreels and Hollywood films? As in most martial societies, indoctrination commenced early with semi-military instruction provided in what we would now call primary school. The reality was that, when compulsory military service for individuals commenced at a later age, each male child had already been imbued with a considerable amount of training, was familiar with, and had usually internalised, military-style discipline. This was in a society where all males between the ages of 17 and 45 were at any time liable for call-up for compulsory military training and service.

Those aged from 17 to 19 were not automatically inducted into the military but were required to undergo basic training. Once a male turned 19, he was given a physical examination to classify him for 'appropriate allocation'.

Not physically large by modern standards, to be classified 'A-1' required a height of at least 5 feet (152 cm) and good health. Those under this height, but still in good physical condition, were categorised as 'B-1'. Typically, the average Japanese soldier of World War II was small, lightly built, but with great physical endurance. In stature they averaged only 5 feet 3 inches (160 cm) and weighed about 116 to 120 pounds (53–55 kg).

Socially and economically, they varied greatly. From an average group of 100: 31 would be farmers; 30 factory workers; 15 office employees; eight worked for the government; five were schoolteachers; three were fishermen; two were miners; with the balance from assorted professions. Typically, all could read and write Japanese to a proficient level and 15 could also read and write English; such was the general high standard of the Japanese education system. More than two-thirds of recruits came from poor households.

In addition to receiving a standard education in the Western traditional sense, Naka, along with all other children, was exposed to the military indoctrination that was a central part of Japan's martial culture. When he left school at the age of 17 he worked for the shipping trading company Mitsui Bussan Kaisha, attending to the bunkering (refuelling) of shipping vessels. It was while dealing with foreign crews calling into the port that he developed and improved his English language skills.

However, as was prescribed by law, the civilian now turned recruit was inducted into the armed forces. This event was a special day for all young men and by tradition was on 10 January each year, the anniversary of the date that the conscription law had originally been enacted. The induction ceremony was a major communal event and provided a great opportunity for the recruit's family, the local community and the armed forces to celebrate the symbolic importance of this occasion. The celebrations would typically involve rousing bands, parades of recruits, and military speeches stressing sacred service to the emperor.

The event also acted as a solemn leave-taking from the family unit, the central pillar of traditional Asian societies emphasising that the commanding officer would now take the place of mother, father and family. Before recruitment, letters would be written to each family stressing this powerful point and asking for personal details about the new recruit. While about 75 per cent of these conscripts would have already had some form of military training, they were all about to enter upon a much tougher, almost Spartan, existence.

Before the war, training of the typical Japanese infantry soldier took 12 months, a standard training period that is to this day mirrored generally across all military forces worldwide. This yearlong process involved initial recruit training, followed with 'corps' training when selected for a specialist area such as signals, artillery or engineering. Once war in Asia commenced, training was subsequently reduced to three months, as also occurred amongst Allied nations, and was further reduced to between six and seven weeks towards the end of World War II.

Training was harsh and punitive and designed to grind down the recruit's individuality and remove free will and any querying of orders and authority. It was devised to create a fighting force that was physically durable, resilient, merciless and unquestioning. The yearlong recruit training program consisted of a series of gradual toughening-up exercises involving marksmanship (for obscure reasons, Japanese soldiers were never renowned for being crack-shots, even after training) and bayonet drill, considered a central part of military strategy.

Naka, along with the other recruits in his group, had his endurance hardened with a series of arduous five-day cross-country marches. These marches increased in intensity over time with an emphasis on physical toughness and the ability to endure the privations of extended field exercises under relentless stress with little sleep or rest. At this point night fighting, highly prized by the Japanese Army, was introduced and bizarrely the soldiers were issued with darkened glasses to wear during the day so as to simulate fighting in dark-night conditions, even wearing them when the moon was full. Two drills a week were now spent on night-fighting training. Naka and his fellow recruits were taught to crawl silently through a training field, by stuffing paper in ammunition pouches, ensuring water canteens were always full, and wrapping rags around any items likely to rattle and create noise. As Naka's skills improved and the year progressed, he and his colleagues took part in major army manoeuvres, often taking place under the watchful eye of the emperor for whom all military glory was ostensibly dedicated.

The one constant and harrowing feature of each soldier's training in the army was the systematic brutalisation of the individual. In all of the Imperial Japanese forces, young recruit soldiers, sailors and airmen were bashed, slapped, kicked and ritualistically humiliated on a regular basis and as an integral part of their training. Even the smallest infringement would result in disciplinary action, often involving corporal punishment. One World War II veteran recounted incidents where a sergeant or corporal would take a dislike to the way a recruit drank his tea and would then order or personally bash the hapless conscript. Another recruit related an episode where he had his belongings stolen and upon reporting this to his sergeant was subsequently beaten by the officer. The consequences and perceived benefits of this cruel and extreme training system were that each soldier learned quickly to obey all orders in an instant and in an unquestioning, reflexive manner. The perverse result was to create the most formidable and efficient soldiers in World War II.

Because Naka had finished middle school, he was eligible for and sat the Officers' Examination which he passed; but he was still required to undertake the rigorous training required of all soldiers. From July to December 1940 he continued his training and military duties in occupied southern China at Bun Chuzan, Nanning, Lang Son in Indo-China and, a little later, Shanghai. During his time there, the Japanese Army's occupation of areas in China resulted in huge military and civilian casualties, numerous war crimes and large-scale destruction and appropriation of property. In December 1940, Naka returned to Japan to begin training for Officers' School and, in August 1941, successfully graduated as a probationary officer. In this position he was now expected to live, eat and suffer the same privations as the men under his command. Naka would find that, as an early graduate, he was somewhat different to the newer, less experienced officers who, as the war progressed and casualties mounted, would be drawn largely from the lower middle class.

Allied propaganda at the time stated of the average Japanese soldier that: 'his posture is poor, his gait is shuffling, teeth in poor condition and often protruding'. This stereotype of the Japanese soldier was designed to establish a negative, contemptuous image in the mind of Allied troops. It mirrored a number of similar attitudes and prejudices held by Westerners.

Japanese short-sightedness, inability to see in the dark, general lack of coordination, and lack of physical prowess were largely unquestioned by Westerners. One bizarre incident involved the Japanese difficulty in purchasing from foreign countries aircraft for Japan's first aircraft carriers. A commentator in Britain said that the sales would be pointless as the Japanese would never be able to fly the planes properly because they were such (supposedly) poor horseriders! Most of these stereotypes were far from reality, as many rueful Allied commanders were soon to discover to their detriment.

In the field, Japanese soldiers were trained to quickly respond to the needs of their comrades and to be willing to share any good fortune, such as the spoils of war, with them. Personal honesty was stressed as was the need to avoid exaggerations, lies and boastfulness. Each individual soldier was to take good care of their health and look after their armaments, equipment and unit horses.

As soldiers, they were taught to suppress their emotions, doubts and fears and to only act for the strategic advancement of their group and their military objective—to ultimately win each battle and the war. Paradoxically, as ingrained as this emphasis on self-discipline, denial and collective glory was, Allied intelligence soon identified that major war crimes by the Japanese—looting, rape, and a range of other military offences—were not at all rare or isolated. Individually and in groups, Japanese soldiers committed numerous acts of robbery, sexual assault, destruction of civilian areas, and large-scale atrocities. So widespread were these crimes, that historians have no doubt that they constituted a general and approved *modus operandi* of the Japanese Army whilst in the field and away from their home islands.

Japanese soldiers scored highly in the Allies' eyes in regards to their courage, strength, hardiness and preparedness to sustain almost sacrificial combat losses without flinching. This meant that, even when they took huge casualties, Japanese commanders maintained their agreed assault plan whereas Allied and Axis forces would either abandon an attack or at least modify it. While this single-minded rigidity and fanatical loyalty was a strength early in the war, which added to the myth of Japanese invincibility, over time it proved an inherent strategic weakness. Simply put, if a plan failed, the attack would more than likely be repeated without alteration until either victory or complete decimation.

The inflexible, unquestioning nature of military training in the Japanese forces generally meant that, throughout the war, when an unforeseen circumstance arose, Japanese officers were often unable or unwilling to make adjustments or countenance changing tactics. On some occasions, Japanese troops simply panicked when confronted with unorthodox strategies or unexpected manoeuvres by opposing forces or even by the miscarriage of their own plans.

Conversely, while individual soldiers were seen to be incredibly tough and resilient, they were also viewed as being unimaginative and slow to improvise. This in no way suggested that the Japanese solider lacked intelligence, but rather related to his rigid basic training and fear of repercussions for not following orders. The Japanese still preferred the fanatical and fearless bayonet charge, as their drilling had emphasised this type of combat and they believed they were superior in its use. This belief also stemmed from their confidence that the ancient samurai tradition of the lone warrior was embodied in each individual soldier which was now being brought to the modern battlefield.

Myths also abounded concerning the ability of the Japanese soldier to survive on just the rice he found whilst in the field. Napoleon's dictum that 'a soldier travels on his stomach' was true for the Japanese too. When he was hungry, he was as dejected as any other soldier. Japanese liked regular meals with variety and, when that was not possible, they became as disheartened and depressed as any other army. When rations were scarce, one soldier wrote in his diary: 'If I eat tonight, I may not be able to eat tomorrow.' The American observers noted that the standard rations for the Japanese soldier were adequate and, after inspection, could easily sustain Allied troops. Rice was a staple but was supplemented by miso soup (similar in taste to Vegemite in hot water or to soy sauce). The deficiency disease beri-beri, caused by a lack of Vitamin B1, could be warded off by adding barley or a few pickled plums to the rice. A side benefit of this addition to their diet was the mild laxative effect that counteracted constipation caused by constant service rations. Japanese soldiers were also issued with the hard biscuits that are seemingly a standard 'punishment' for soldiers of all nations!

Soldiers lucky to be in a base camp enjoyed a canteen, where they could (allowing for cultural differences) purchase many of the same items available to Allied soldiers: sake, beer, cigarettes, canned milk, sweets, sweet biscuits, canned fruit, canned crab and salmon, and clothing such as socks and underpants, toothpaste, soap, pens, writing paper and so on.

Like most Japanese infantrymen, Maseo Naka was well armed and well equipped with the best kit his country could produce. Although Japan had only recently industrialised, it had learned quickly and could manufacture good-quality and functional armaments and, subject to some exceptions, their design and operation was first-class. An exception was the 'Model 94' pistol issued to officers. Low-powered, ungainly and unreliable, it was said to be more dangerous to the operator than the target!

For the Japanese military machine, scale and capacity were always their persistent problem. Japanese leaders were fatally deluded in thinking that they could ever match America's industrial might which was 50 per cent of world capacity by war's end. Historians have estimated that, even at its height, Japan had at best, approximately 10 per cent of America's industrial capacity during World War II and for that reason alone it was destined to lose.

As a fighting force in prepared positions, the resistance of Japanese soldiers was fanatical. No fighting force generally likes to be in a static position as it is always vulnerable to sustained attack and will ultimately fall to a force which escalates the ways and means to overcome military obstacles. The Japanese soldier's ability and determination to defend a prepared position was seen not only in bloody battles like on the Pacific island of Guadalcanal but *in extremis* in defence of the Japanese island of Iwo Jima. The huge and almost incomprehensible Japanese armed forces and civilian casualties in this invasion was one of the major reasons why Allied commanders approved the use of the atomic bombs on Hiroshima and Nagasaki to end the war. Put quite simply, the USA was not prepared to incur estimates of several hundred thousand deaths that would be necessary to conquer the Japanese homeland islands.

For the Japanese soldier, therefore, surrender under any and all circumstances was considered a profound disgrace to himself, to his family, his comrades and, ultimately, to his emperor. 'Fight hard' recruits were told time and again, and 'if you are afraid in battle, you will die, if you are not afraid, you will not die. Under no circumstances become a straggler or a prisoner of war. If you become helpless, commit suicide nobly.'

These were the soldiers, among them Maseo Naka, that the Allies were about to encounter in New Guinea.

CHAPTER 4

NEW GUINEA

Japanese soldiers who had been fighting in southern China for nearly a decade were battle-hardened, ruthless and resilient. However, they had little or no experience in the unique challenges of jungle warfare until their seemingly inexorable sweep through French Indochina (modern Vietnam, Laos and Cambodia), Malaya, Burma and the Philippines.

The ultimate test of their temperament, fortitude and resolve was in New Guinea where their already stretched lines of supply now snaked more than 3,000 miles (5,000 km) from Japan's home islands. The alien and impenetrable jungle, isolation from supplies and command posts, mountainous terrain and hostile and dogged Australian forces made the fighting in New Guinea some of the most desperate in the Pacific War.

The jungle conditions affected Japanese soldiers both physically and psychologically; the heat, humidity, mud and rain meant that their ammunition and the traditional infantry soldier's kit of leather began to rust and rot soon after arrival. Despite their battle-readiness, the Japanese as well as the Allies had no great affection for this new battlefield of light and shade, impenetrable undergrowth and near vertical ascents. While the Japanese adapted quickly as soldiers, this unfamiliar landscape became the real enemy in the long run due to that absolute war necessity: consistent, ordered and responsive supply lines. The Allies struggled with similar issues, although they had the industrial might of the United States, supported by the increasing capacity of the Australian war economy. With the survival of the nation at stake, the Allies were determined to ensure that their troops had the tools for victory. Before the Americans arrived in New Guinea to relieve and support the Australians, 1942 was a desperate and lonely time for the part-time militia and Australian Imperial Force (AIF) soldiers battling the Japanese back and forth in the mountainous jungle with its permanent twilight of mist and rain. The relieving American soldiers initially felt that victory would be easy and quick, but overconfidence from the first units into battle soon produced the opposite effect—instances of reluctance to engage and even avoidance of the enemy. The Americans lacked combat experience in jungle warfare and quickly realised they were in trouble. They soon formed solid partnerships with the Australians with their greater experience in this form of warfare and then drew upon their allies' toughness and invaluable expertise. Postwar American accounts of these partnerships, particularly the authoritative work *Victory in Papua*, praises the Australians as 'true partners' in the desperate fighting that, for the first time during the Pacific War, saw the Japanese turned back and ultimately defeated on the battlefield. The Japanese, while quick to adapt to jungle fighting, were ultimately defeated by the unique and challenging landscape so memorably described by a number of war correspondents in New Guinea at the time.

One of these early observers was New Zealand journalist Osmar White who reported that the first adversary for the Japanese invading forces was likely to be the difficult terrain. The main island of New Guinea, located deep in the southern tropics, is shaped rather like a rearing dragon with a near impenetrable 'spine' of steep mountains running east to west across the island about 1,600 km (1,000 miles) long. The environment ranges from extremes of snow-capped peaks, vine-laden rainforests, to steaming, stinking leech-ridden swamps. From the backbone of this mountain range, rows of steep ridges string out like ribs. These are fed with arteries of flowing mountain torrents from the constant rain and all clothed in the everlasting rain clouds. The extremes of this climate were so inhospitable that, despite their youth and extreme fitness, elite American paratroopers who were landed in the kunai grass of the Ramu and Markham Rivers collapsed within one hour, such were the excesses of heat and humidity. Not only was the weather their adversary, but debilitating pests and diseases also abounded in the cloistered humidity. Medical reports found men succumbing to malaria, typhus, hookworm and yaws (a tropical infection of the skin, bones and joints). Topping this bewildering range of ailments off were a range of skin diseases of unimaginable variety. The devastating effects on soldiers of enduring combat conditions for long periods in this climate had been clearly identified in Australia from its World War I experiences. Australia's official history of that conflict, the first Australian combat of World War I, noted that 'the country is one for men between twenty five and forty years of age and the insidious climate fastens relentlessly on any physical weakness.' While previously, attitude and training were considered the main attributes of a fighting force, World War I confirmed that only seasoned, healthy men of robust fitness could be depended upon in these combat situations. Even then, none but elite troops could last more than a few days of strenuous effort.

After World War II, White along with others examined the controversy over whether Japan planned to invade Australia (if they had defeated the Allied forces in New Guinea). Japan may have faced few impediments with an initial invasion, but only if they had limited themselves to parts of northern Australia. Certainly, Rabaul's defences were feeble, with some old Hudson bombers, a few obsolete Wirraway 'fighters' (which were no more than training aircraft) and just 1400 Australian soldiers with inadequate artillery. The story was completely refuted by Dr Peter Stanley in his article, '"He's (not) coming south": the invasion that wasn't', which showed that while the idea was discussed, it never featured in any Japanese war plans and was in fact condemned as a concept because it would stretch Japanese resources too far. Rather than invade, Japan's plan was to isolate Australia.

The initial Japanese successes in attacking Malaya, the Philippines and the East Indies (modern Indonesia) were surprising not only in their realisation but in their strategy. While Japan had slavishly copied much of the European powers' military structures, it had also created something unique in its own tactical movements. Here, for the first time, was an army that comprised an 'aero amphibious' assault structure that seamlessly coordinated all elements in a successful landing. Once disembarked, its soldiers required less food, shelter, transport, leadership and generally less support than the fighters of almost any other army. Because of their brutal training and indoctrination, the fear of death and wounding was virtually eliminated. Their soldiers were therefore tougher than the Allied armies at this point and also less susceptible to privations and disease. The Japanese High Command based their ambitious plans and strategies on this advantage following the maxim: 'How can we get what we want with what we have!' This unswerving resolve and strength had been an advantage up this point in the war, but would eventually become a weakness. But for the AIF and militia units about to face them in New Guinea, this was an enemy to be reckoned with.

Maseo Naka's military journey from Japan to New Guinea was a long and circuitous one and the complete story of this odyssey was fully revealed in his later interrogation after his capture. Naka was one of the majority of Japanese men conscripted into the armed forces immediately they turned 21. He entered the army in April 1940 and was posted to the 41st Infantry Regiment Depot Unit in Fukuyama as a second class private. The 41st was an established old unit that had been based in Fukuyama in the Hiroshima Prefecture since the Meiji Restoration in the 1860s. Fukuyama had historically been a small coastal village famous for traditional net fishing of sea bream and had later grown to become a major commercial port. The area was regarded as having a mild climate protected from the ravages of typhoons (cyclones) by the surrounding hills. It later developed into an administrative centre for the surrounding area featuring weaving mills and a flourishing rice industry.

In September 1940, Naka was posted to Lang Son in French Indochina[5] and then to Shanghai, China, where he stayed for one month, later returning to Japan to enter the Officers' Training School. He graduated from there in August 1941 and was posted back to China. Naka's army pay was 140 Yen a month and he was also given a one-off allowance of 400 Yen to purchase specific items needed by an officer. He later complained that his allowance was insufficient. As an officer, he was allowed to keep items already issued to him but, if he wanted a sword or a pistol, he had to purchase them himself, so he opted for a sword but not a pistol.

5 In 1940, Japan occupied French Indochina following agreement with the French Vichy government.

In November 1941 in the weeks preceding Pearl Harbor, his unit sailed from Ningpo (Ningbo), China to Malaya where it attacked on 8 December 1941, the day of the surprise attack on the American Pacific Fleet at Hawaii. The Japanese forces relentlessly pursued the retreating Allies south until stunningly securing the surrender of Singapore, the 'Gibraltar of the East' on 15 February 1942. Japan appeared unstoppable. It had attacked Pearl Harbor, Hong Kong, Malaya, Thailand and Burma on 7–8 December 1941.[6] The first Borneo landings were on 10 December with the Philippines attacked on 16 December. These attacks were all part of a plan originally hatched as part of Japanese naval strategy. First, attack and weaken the US Navy at Hawaii; allow it to regroup; let it sail for the Philippines in an effort to retake it from the Japanese and then subject it to a massive counterstrike that would destroy it. Unfortunately such plans have too many contingencies and the flaw was that in this process General MacArthur took himself and his command to Australia rather than Hawaii, so the US Fleet did not behave as supposed. The Japanese realised that rather than the USA allowing Japan to stay in control of the South-East Asia area it was taking a stand much closer than first envisaged and so waging war from a united USA and Australasian Allied force.

Naka's victorious unit (now known as Yazawa Butai[7]) left Singapore on 25 March 1942 and docked at Lingayen as part of the invasion of the Philippines, an American protectorate, where Naka was hospitalised with fever. His unit left without him for the island of Panay but he rejoined it at the city of Davao in April where they fought against combined American and Filipino forces. Resistance from both local and American forces took Japan far longer to overcome than first anticipated. While the Philippines required more troops and time to overpower, the Allies knew that it would only be a matter of weeks before New Guinea would be next in line for invasion with the island of New Britain the likely base for the attack. The island of New

6 Pearl Harbor was east of the International Date Line so for the United States it was officially a day earlier on 7 December 1941.

7 Japanese unit names were altered with changes in commanders.

Guinea, an Australian League of Nations protectorate since World War I, was fiercely inhospitable and most Australians knew little about it. Expatriate Australians and Europeans that had some knowledge of this primitive island were quickly 'rounded up' to face a friendly but unrelenting inquisition on every known fact about the region.

Japan had to abandon its invasion plans for New Caledonia, Samoa and Fiji after it had been defeated at the sea battle of Midway in June 1942 but it still had plans to take and occupy the capital of New Guinea at Port Moresby. Controlling New Guinea would isolate Australia and so reduce America's effectiveness in the South Pacific. Major General Tomitaro Horii's South Sea Force was designated to undertake the capture of Port Moresby. His main body of troops was stationed in Rabaul on the island of New Britain and redeployed from there on 17 August 1942 to the north coast of the New Guinea mainland. Naka's 41st Regiment, together with battalions of the 144th and engineers and dismounted cavalry and mountain gunners, struck the Kokoda Track leading from the north coast to Port Moresby on the south along the axis represented by the Deniki Isurava track and spur.

The fighting against the Australian defenders did not reach its definitive phase until the 2nd and 3rd Battalions of Naka's 41st Regiment arrived to join the battle. The 1st Battalion (including Naka's platoon), having landed later, joined the battle along with 1,000 fresh Japanese troops. General Horii now had the equivalent of two brigades and alternated in using them in the advance against the Australians. Even though combat and sickness casualties depleted his strength daily, he still had 5,000 fighting men available on 12 September. Shortly after this time his forces suffered a number of serious reverses from Australian and American air attacks and from the chronic effects of their supply lines being overstretched. The defeat of Japanese forces at Milne Bay on the eastern tip of New Guinea was a significant blow, but the Japanese High Command was intent on retaking both Milne Bay and the island of Guadalcanal in the Solomon Islands. Horii's men were ordered to fall back to the Buna Gona area on the north coast which was a more easily defended position as well as an obvious place for an Allied landing.

The Japanese believed that, once Guadalcanal and Milne Bay were retaken, Major General Horii could recommence the march to Port Moresby. Except for the 2nd Battalion, the 41st were retreating to Buna with the 144th. The 41st's job was to fight a rearguard action against the Australians. The 2nd Battalion had the job of protecting the Japanese rear. When the bulk of the 41st had made it to their objective, the Australians struck their main blow against the remaining Japanese at Ioribaiwa on the Kokoda Track on 28 September 1942.

There has been longstanding tension between survivors of this campaign from the 41st Regiment and those of the 144th. Veterans of the 144th accused the 41st of failing them on a number of occasions. One incident particularly incensed the 144th, that being the 41st's failure to carry out their orders to protect the rear of the 144th as they retreated on 10–11 November 1942. Accounts suggest that it did not even attempt to carry out this command and instead immediately struck out for the Kumusi River on the northern side of the Kokoda Track where they escaped to the Japanese side, thereby abandoning most of their rifles and equipment.

In their defence, the 41st had been an elite unit, having successfully fought campaigns in China, taken part in garrison work in Indochina, been involved in the attack on Malaya and the taking of Singapore (where it met the Australians for the first time), and fought in the Philippines. In New Guinea, it had arrived as a late addition to the South Pacific Force and was often held in reserve with only two out of the three battalions actually in New Guinea with the other remaining in New Britain. It should also be remembered that inter-unit rivalry is common to all armed forces and blame-shifting, condemnation and obfuscation are particular features in Japan's collective memory of World War II.

Whatever the ultimate cause, the Australians now pursued the Japanese relentlessly back across the Kokoda Track. On 10 November 1942, the Allies captured the camp at Oivi and pushed on finally towards Giruwa and Basabua on the north coast. Fresh Allied troops landed to the south of Buna but the Japanese were intent on repelling them. The Americans bombarded the Buna area on 16 November with

Naka and the remnants of the 41st crossing the Kumusi River near Pinga and arriving in the Gona area. The main part of the regiment was now unfit for sustained battle. They had no provisions and were so desperately fatigued that many of the troops had simply thrown their weapons away. Naka's platoon now had just 50 rifles and one heavy machine gun. Under increasingly desperate fighting, they were deployed near Kigoku and then withdrew to Napapo on 13 December to around 3 km north-west of Gona. The sick and wounded were set up in makeshift hospitals but were almost immediately berated by their officers and ordered to crawl from their beds (there were no beds) and fight with sticks and clubs until they died. This well-disciplined army, so imbued with military fervour, had been reduced to such a state!

The main Australian unit that was in the area close to Naka was the 55/53, a composite militia battalion. After Buna and Gona were captured, the Australian 16th Brigade attacked one of the final Japanese bridge heads in New Guinea on the north coast at Sananda but found this heavy going, suffering significant casualties. The action involved the 55/53 and two other battalions being moved into the assault and, early on 7 December, making a small attack against Japanese positions to divert enemy attention from the main attack against Sananda. The battalion continued patrolling to draw fire from the Japanese and deplete their ammunition. In their thankless role as decoys, the battalion suffered causalities of 108 men killed or wounded. More aggressive patrolling followed but, once again, the Australians could not penetrate the Japanese defences. The 55/53 was finally relieved in early January 1943 and moved to a new position at Gona. Sananda was not completely cleared and captured until 21 January 1943.

Naka's official prisoner of war record shows that he was captured on 27 January 1943. The 55/53 Battalion war diary, being the only Australian unit in the area, indicates that just one prisoner[8] was captured around that time on 26 January. The entry stated the 55/53

8 While it is an assumption that it was Campbell who captured Naka, it is the most sound considering the official records investigated to date.

Battalion's 24-year-old Lieutenant Lyle Campbell proceeded to the battalion area and, on the way in, captured a Japanese prisoner who was handed over to the brigade intelligence officer. Naka had been spotted by Campbell's patrol. He was seen semi-comatose under scrub, shaking with fever, filthy and starving. Naka was hauled to his feet and taken back to the battalion. His records showed he weighed just 39 kg. The 55/53 Infantry Battalion continued to be heavily involved in operations around Buna and Gona before the handover to American forces. It returned to Port Moresby at the end of January. Later in New Guinea, Campbell suffered a bout of malaria and was sent back to Australia, later training at Canungra in October 1944.[9] He continued his service with British forces in Burma and in Britain.

The day after Naka's capture, the new Japanese regimental commander, Major Koiwai Mitsuo arrived at the mouth of the Kumusi River to take command of the regimental flag. What was left of the 41st Infantry Regiment was withdrawn to Rabaul in mid-June 1943 and was later sent to Korea in September 1943. But Maseo Naka was not with them, he was a prisoner in the hands of the Allies. The life of the regiment went on without him. He was now only spoken of in the past tense. To his friends, family and comrades, he was dead.

9 Thirty years later to the month the author was in the same camp in Southern Queensland.

CHAPTER 5
NEVER BE A PRISONER

So that we may have a better understanding of Maseo Naka and his fellow prisoners of war, it is important to spend some time looking at the Japanese view of capture at that time.

Westerners have a general understanding from popular culture of Japanese soldiers as prisoners of war: embittered, humiliated fanatics hell-bent on escape or death!

But the reality was even stranger. Officers and men of the Imperial Japanese forces in fact never saw capture as even a remote possibility. In simple terms, the Japanese soldier could never surrender, not under any circumstances. For him, it was the 'Banzai' charge using his rifle with its lethal bayonet as the modern incarnation of the samurai sword. If he could not win the day and stay alive, he would die honourably in battle.

Even before he became a soldier, it was well understood in martial Japanese culture that one should never be captured alive. A number of studies on soldiers who have been captured all highlight the corrosive effects, emotionally, psychologically and physically, of imprisonment. Men of action and adventurous spirit, stripped of motivation and status, often wither and fade. While a criminal views imprisonment as an occupational hazard, a soldier views it as the ultimate failing in their mission, hence the historical obsession of most prisoners of war with escape. For the Japanese soldier, this sense of shame was compounded and reinforced many times over. The Japanese Government produced a number of edicts over the years before and during World War II stressing the doctrine that being taken a prisoner was the most heinous crime imaginable. Whatever the circumstances and whatever the situation, it was emphasised that a Japanese soldier, sailor or airman could never be exonerated for such a violation.[10] The policy confirmed that any Japanese who committed this offence would be executed upon their return to Japan.

The consequences of capture also flowed onto the families of potential prisoners of war, doubly distressing for soldiers from a traditionally Asian, family-oriented society. In the event of defeat, soldiers were told to commit suicide quickly or as soon as practicable. To understand how all-encompassing and pervasive this edict was, there is evidence of a Japanese officer having committed suicide as a result of losing a pre-World War II 'mock battle' during war games, such was the sense of dishonour at defeat! Another anecdote claims that the shame for one junior lieutenant was so overpowering that he committed suicide after making a mistake whilst reading the Emperor's Imperial Rescript to fellow soldiers. The evidence of this edict's deadly and overpowering effect on the behaviour of officers and men is illustrated by the fact that only 39,000 Japanese servicemen surrendered in the entire Pacific War out of an armed forces of more than seven million. In contrast, the Germans took more than 600,000 Soviet prisoners during just one battle in the Russian Ukraine in 1941.

Compare this to the bloody invasion of the island of Iwo Jima in early 1945 in which the invading Americans suffered 3,500 dead. More startling though is the fact that, out of a total of 21,000 Japanese soldiers defending the island, only 216 surrendered; the rest were either killed or committed suicide. Later in 1945 on the Japanese homeland island of Okinawa, thousands of Japanese civilians, men, women and children, threw themselves into American gunfire armed only with farm implements, or simply committed suicide.

In the battle for New Guinea in 1942–43 more than 16,000 Japanese soldiers died with just 328 taken prisoner; on the island of Bougainville, 16,500 Japanese died with just 230 captured. As the Japanese military code expressly forbade capture, all Japanese military personnel were instructed that should seizure by enemy forces be

---

10 Even pilots and aircrew were not normally issued with parachutes and, if they were, often chose not to use them but rather to fly their dying aircraft for one last act.

imminent, they were to save the last bullet for themselves or charge at the enemy in a suicidal assault. The Allied forces were also extremely cautious in accepting surrender from the Japanese, as a number of Allied soldiers had been killed by Japanese soldiers detonating concealed hand grenades and other explosive devices or weapons. The USA's official history of the war offered the following euphemism on the overall small number of Japanese prisoners, stating that some: 'may not have survived the heat of combat'. There is no doubt that for the Australians in New Guinea who had previously fought in the Middle East, there was a greater enthusiasm for killing Japanese than they had for Germans or Italians. Australian commanders in the North African campaigns had lamented that, in spite of overall military successes, they had great trouble in fully developing a killer instinct against the enemy. There was no such 'problem' in New Guinea. War correspondents in the South Pacific campaigns often expressed their reports in terms of Australians 'hunting down' and 'exterminating Japanese'. It was in every way an unrelenting and merciless campaign on both sides.

Another illustration of this reluctance to surrender was evidenced during the Allies' island-hopping strategy designed to bypass non-strategic enemy strongholds in 1944–45. This strategy meant that isolated Japanese forces were often left behind enemy lines in what was now Allied territory. The remaining Japanese forces were pursued around these islands, assisted in part by captured Japanese soldiers who helped prepare leaflets in Japanese, English and Pidgin that offered safe passage. These leaflets were dropped into areas where Japanese soldiers were known to be holding out. The original version of this leaflet stated that the person holding the handbill had 'surrendered'. That word, said the cooperating Japanese, was not acceptable and would not produce the desired result. After some considerable internal discussion it was agreed that the new version of the leaflet would instead say 'ceased resistance' rather than 'surrendered'. Even after the war, a Japanese author described a surrendered officer and 50 of his men as 'disarmed soldiers'. For the few Japanese who were captured, the reasons for their ceasing resistance or surrendering varied considerably. Some ordinary soldiers became angry and disillusioned at officers who had stolen food supplies for their own use; others witnessed the immense firepower of the Allies and saw the futility of further combat. Some simply wanted to live, and others admitted to shooting their officers dead so that they could surrender. Total numbers surrendering were a tiny fraction of all Japanese military forces.

The tragedy of war is in the fact that, in the end, soldiers are just people, even those who have been indoctrinated into a warrior supremacy myth as occurred with the Axis powers during World War II. An example of this disconnect between the illusion and the reality of the Japanese soldier's single-minded fanaticism was revealed during one experience with prisoners of war. The interrogator asked them if it was true that all dying Japanese soldiers shouted 'Long live the Emperor' as their last words. The response was unexpected; they said that maybe one in 10,000 or even one in 20,000 would scream the phrase, 'Tenno Heika Banzai' but mostly what they heard soldiers crying out, they said, was simply the word 'mother'.

If a Japanese surrendered, the results could be extremely personal. The family of a Japanese pilot captured at Milne Bay in New Guinea (who subsequently died in the Cowra breakout) was almost run out of their village when it became known that their son had surrendered. As this anecdote illustrates, the shame of capture for the family of a prisoner of war would and did result in many forms of retribution, including the loss of a job or refusal to marry an eligible daughter from such a family—in short, genuine and severe ostracism. Such was the power of vengeance in a group-oriented society that this indoctrination also impacted negatively on Japanese attitudes towards Allied troops who had surrendered.

Nevertheless, a number of Japanese soldiers when facing death acted differently to the expected norm of sacrificing their life for their emperor. Many of these individuals had come to the conclusion that the war was lost and that they could better serve their country and their family if they lived. Their logic went: how can I help Japan if I kill myself?

These were the few thousand who had not simply been captured while severely wounded or who were left behind by their units either exhausted, starving, sick or delirious, but that had actively surrendered to the Allied forces. For this small group, what happened after their surrender amazed them. In total contrast to the grotesque propaganda from their own military on the supposed treatment of Japanese prisoners, the Allies did not kill or torture them. In fact, to their complete shock, their captors gave them cigarettes, food, water, shelter and medical treatment equal to that afforded to their own soldiers. These unexpected acts of kindness greatly affected many of these Japanese prisoners who had been taught to fear and hate the Allies, which possibly explains the subsequent change of attitude in many of the prisoners of war. Acts of kindness in traditional Asian societies are normally expected to be reciprocated, and this humane treatment from their enemy seemed to impose a moral obligation on a number of the Japanese to cooperate and assist the Allies in an effort to repay this goodwill.

Naka was now one of these prisoners in that small select group of Japanese who had 'ceased resistance', meaning that they had surrendered. Yet Naka could genuinely claim that he had not surrendered or even ceased resistance. Like many Japanese soldiers taken prisoner, he had simply collapsed from exhaustion and hunger. He was found lying alone and unconscious in the jungle, spotted by chance by patrolling Australian soldiers who thought they had seen just 'another dead Jap' until he moved after being poked in the ribs. Like many Australian soldiers in dealing with the Japanese, they were rough but not cruel, going through his pockets and checking for grenades, knives and anything else that might be used against them. They found nothing and no other weapons could be seen. Naka's sword and rifle had long since been discarded. Dragged to his feet, he half stumbled, half walked back to the 55/53 Battalion's camp where he would stay under guard before being transferred for second-stage interrogation. While under the watch of the Australians, he was given both Australian and American rations with doctors and other medical staff attending to him while he remained in a blur of lost time and consciousness. Waking finally from a period of fitful, feverish sleep, he became aware of his surroundings and was amazed to find that he was still alive.

For a soldier reared in the strict martial monoculture of Imperial Japan, this was like landing on another planet with strange-looking people with different coloured skin walking around him, unusually dressed and speaking English, of which some he could understand. Stranger still, these were the hated enemy but they were looking after and attending to him; he was not dead and he was ashamed. He could see white and black faces around him: Australians and locals. Some Papuan 'Fuzzy Wuzzy' native bearers[11] were standing close by, staring down at him. He looked up and the guards had a joke: 'Look out, they might eat you!' Two guards turned up next to the camp stretcher he was on. 'Up' they ordered and the bearers took the weight of the stretcher poles and headed off.

By 8 February 1943 Naka, his body wracked by malaria, was finding it hard going on the primitive winding tracks while being transferred to Port Moresby. The journey was awful, being transported by rugged American jeeps tearing over the rough and bone-shaking roads. He would fall asleep for just a few minutes at a time, then wake before drifting back into semi-consciousness.

Naka was a severely troubled man; he was now starting to remember that he had been in command of a platoon of between 13 and 15 men and he knew in his heart that they were all likely dead. Were they all dead or still alive in the jungle? His captors told him nothing, but he couldn't stop thinking about his duty to them. When he fell asleep, he muttered their names and the words, 'I've lost all my men.' In true Bushido tradition, he knew that he must die by taking his own life. His sense of shame and failure was a torment worse than death. He believed that he heard his family crying out 'You must die soon' and his response 'But how am I going to do it?'

Naka's interrogation followed the procedures and script established by the US Allied Translator and Intelligence Service which were designed to elicit as much useful intelligence as the prisoner of war (POW) could provide without making them believe that they had

11 The native bearers were referred to at the time as 'Fuzzy Wuzzy Angels', partly because of their hair but mainly because they were instrumental in carrying wounded allies from the battlefield to field hospitals.

betrayed their comrades and country. While this questioning was underway, Naka came into regular contact with more and more of the Australian sentries. He noted that most of the guards were old soldiers from World War I who, unlike their Japanese counterparts, were genuinely friendly with a touching sense of humour. They asked Naka what he would do when he got back to Japan after the war and he replied that he would not be going back and would most likely be dead.

'When you become healthy, and the war ends, you can go back home where your family is waiting for you, as an honourable prisoner of war.'

'The Japanese do not have a word for "honourable prisoners of war",' he interjected. 'Therefore, the only thing left for me is the choice of when to die.'

But his guards pointed out that he had been ill, had become unconscious, and had only been saved by the enemy while one step away from death. It was natural and inevitable, they said, that he had been captured. Had he not given enough loyalty to his country with nothing to be ashamed of? What could he achieve if he died, they asked? He could only serve his country again if he lived!

Naka knew that the Australian guards must have lost many colleagues and friends in World War I and may even have had sons fighting now, and yet they were still showing compassion and respect to an enemy combatant. He wondered if Japanese soldiers in the same position would have acted in a similar way, or whether they would have sought revenge for their dead comrades, which had so often been the case with victorious Japanese forces. He began to understand that, for the Australians, captured Japanese soldiers were no longer their enemies but were in fact praised for their bravery. Years later many ex-prisoners of war would say: 'I started to feel ashamed of our narrow-mindedness as Japanese.'

Like many of the Japanese prisoners, Naka began to experience a profound and deeply affecting personal conflict. On the one hand, he had a strong measure of personal courage like the majority of his comrades and he knew that because he was a prisoner of war he was bound by duty to commit suicide. As a human being, his natural and first reaction was to survive and as a prisoner he had now been offered a conflicting and different message. That was to survive, get well, and return to Japan after the war where he could continue to serve his country.

There is a parallel story to that of Maseo Naka. Another from the same regiment was a Masaru Moriki. Like Naka, Moriki was captured and transferred to the Cowra Prisoner of War Camp where his time there corresponded to that of Naka. Unlike Naka, Moriki easily settled into the routine of camp life. He seemed to enjoy the handicraft activities, the work details, sumo wrestling, playing mahjong, making wooden thongs, and growing vegetables. But even for him, the old bonds of duty, honour and sacrifice would return. Amongst Moriki and his fellow soldiers there were many melancholy discussions on the theme: 'Because I am a prisoner … my sister may not be able to marry because she is the sister of a prisoner, my brother may be ostracised by others in school, my parents and my elder sister will be made to feel so ashamed…'

Moriki remained at the Cowra camp up to, and was a participant in, the breakout in August 1944.

CHAPTER 6
INTERROGATE THE ENEMY

Naka was flown to the Australian mainland and interned in Queensland at the Gaythorne Prisoner of War Camp on 23 February 1943. His Japanese uniform had rotted from his time in jungle and he now wore a recycled Australian summer uniform. Nearby was the stately old mansion 'Tighnabruaich' in the Brisbane suburb of Indooroopilly where Japanese prisoners were interrogated. Tighnabruaich was originally built in 1892 and named after a district in Scotland; the property was requisitioned from about October 1942 by a joint United States–Australian intelligence unit: the Allied Translator and Interpreter Section (ATIS). Its official name did not reveal its significant interrogation work.

Nisei, ethnic Japanese-Americans, handled much of the translation and interpretation work, together with other personnel who directed the handling of captured Japanese prisoners and documents. Nisei were housed across the Brisbane River in the ATIS Camp called Camp Chelmer which was located in Neilson House, Rosebery Terrace, Chelmer. During the period 1942–43, many huts and tents were assembled on the grounds for use by American and Australian soldiers, along with brick cell blocks and accommodation for Japanese prisoners awaiting interrogation.[12] Naka was about to enter a facility whose carefully calibrated practices were designed by the Americans to extract every piece of information possible from him.

12 After the war, Japanese graffiti on walls in some upstairs rooms was painted over in preparation for the building's sale. The building is reputed to be haunted by the ghost of a Japanese POW who committed suicide at this time.

Because of the small numbers of prisoners actually taken, the Allies carefully prepared each individual for the next step: information gathering. The interrogation was a highly structured process involving the use of psychology to encourage the prisoner to divulge as much useful information as they could. The Allies soon discovered that the mental and emotional journey of a typical Japanese prisoner had three distinct phases. First, prisoners provided little useful information in the first 48 hours of imprisonment due to the trauma of capture and their terrifying fear of torture and execution. Interrogations carried out during this period generally provided only confused and unreliable information. This time was therefore generally used to provide good food, medical treatment, and rest for the prisoners of war.

The second phase of the process occurred with the prisoner's dawning realisation that they were not going to be brutalised or killed. This was the crucial moment that intelligence officers awaited. The prisoner, after having been treated surprisingly well with food, shelter and medical treatment, then usually fell prey to an 'obligation syndrome' where they felt the need to repay their captors. With their initial fears transformed to gratitude, they talked freely. Over the next 10 to 14 days, the prisoners were at their most informative and tended to reveal all that they knew with little or nothing held back.

The third phase of the progression occurred when they developed familiarity with their surroundings and became accustomed to their comfortable conditions. Interrogation at this stage generally only drove them to indifference, with any information they provided becoming increasingly unreliable. The reality was that they had revealed nearly all of the important information that they possessed. Some prisoners looked to further ingratiate themselves and started to fabricate and embellish their knowledge. Any continuation at this point risked corrupting what they had already revealed. At this point they were usually released from interrogation and transferred to a prisoner of war camp for internment.

Interrogation techniques in the early stages of the war were initially far from scientific. Since the enemy were generally Germans, Italians and Japanese, the first requirement for a would-be interrogator was to speak the language of their subject. Therefore, linguists had to learn interrogation techniques and interrogators had to learn the relevant language, the latter being a much more difficult task. Linguists fluent in German and Japanese were rare in Australia and, when recruited, were usually provided 'on-the-job' training by senior personnel who had a flair for questioning techniques. There were few manuals detailing how to conduct an interrogation, so a new inquisitor was placed with an experienced operator and would be mentored and monitored as they learned the techniques.

Japanese captured in New Guinea were subject to an initial interrogation combined with medical treatment. Some of these interrogations necessarily involved eliciting information from dying prisoners. In spite of being the enemy, the interrogators found the questioning of mortally wounded men emotionally draining. As difficult as it was, obtaining information at this crucial juncture of the conflict was deemed more important than giving comfort to a dying man, such is the pitiless nature of war. Techniques used on able-bodied Japanese were necessarily more subtle.

Under the direction of the American military, Hollywood became a major contributor to the war effort. In this role, they produced patriotic and entertaining films and musicals to comfort those at home and serving abroad. As well as these propaganda films, Hollywood also produced a vast array of training films, including interrogation techniques. Some of these productions were light entertainment, but their real job was to promote to the audience a greater understanding and participation in the war effort, as well as to impart the necessary skills to beat the enemy. Well-known actors of the day were involved in these productions, with Burgess Meredith, for example, starring as a trainee in a 25-minute short on training an air gunner. His officer-in-charge in this film was Ronald Reagan, later to become president of the United States.

A training film on interrogation shows a Japanese prisoner standing in front of a desk and being asked a series of questions with the subject only providing his name, rank and serial number. The interrogator interjects with the question: 'I suppose the officers who abandoned you in Guadalcanal, told you that if you were captured by the Allies, that you would be executed? Well, you haven't been, have you?' The interrogator instructs a guard to take him away, feed him well, and provide him with medical treatment. The next day the prisoner is brought back visibly relaxed and thanking his interrogator. He is then advised that the Red Cross will be informed that he is a prisoner with his family notified. 'Oh no please, do not tell the Red Cross,' pleads the prisoner. 'Japanese are ashamed at being captured and my family would be shamed as well.' The interrogator has cleverly manipulated the prisoner's expected reaction; by agreeing not to inform the Red Cross, he has provided a favour to the prisoner who now becomes more compliant.

There was another powerful tool available to ATIS which played on the Japanese soldiers' sense of 'honour'. Often a Japanese prisoner would ask to be allowed to kill themselves. This request was common enough for the Allies to issue special orders that this demand should not be granted as it represented a last-ditch attempt by the prisoner to take control of their situation. When it was denied and the detainee had no further avenues for dying honourably, a remarkable transformation often occurred. The captured soldier would almost immediately discard his extreme nationalistic views and became a model prisoner!

One American official observed that some of the older Japanese hardliners quickly transformed, going to extreme lengths to please their captors. Former fanatics unexpectedly volunteered to identify Japanese ammunition dumps on captured maps, write propaganda for the Allies, and even fly on bombing missions guiding pilots to military targets.[13] The interrogators found that, in many instances, the earlier prisoners told the new ones to disclose all military intelligence that they had to their interrogators so that they would all not be blamed for lying or falsifying information that had been previously supplied. One instance involved a prisoner returning to his interrogators advising them that he had checked some facts with his friends relating to what

13 Arnold Kramer, 'Japanese Prisoners of War in America', *Pacific Historical Review*, Vol 52 No 1 (February 1983), p 73.

he had previously revealed under questioning, and now wished to correct some of the details.

The first job for an interrogator of Japanese prisoners in Australia was to assist in the recording of the interviews that were conducted in a separate room. When prisoners were first brought in, interrogators carried out a selection process of high-value candidates. Those prisoners that were assessed as likely to have information of importance, such as officers, senior non-commissioned officers, warrant officers, and specialists such as signals personnel, would be separated and sent to the Detailed Interrogation Facility at Witten Barracks, Indooroopilly. The sessions were no Spanish Inquisition. They were quite civilised affairs and were mostly held at conversational level.

Arthur Page was one such interrogator.[14] He was born in Japan of Greek-Russian parents with the family moving to Australia just before the attack on Pearl Harbor. This unusual background offered him a unique perspective on the Japanese. He was one of a rare group of Europeans who were not only fluent native speakers of Japanese, but also had grown up there and knew the Japanese people, their customs, much of their way of life, and their psychology. In recounting his extensive career as an interrogator, Page felt that, in dealing with Japanese prisoners, they were most vulnerable at the immediate point of their capture. Following some often rough handling by Australian soldiers and because they were often in such poor physical condition, they were usually quite emotional and anxious. Interrogators never resorted to physical abuse or threats as this was considered to be totally counterproductive.

There were only a few trained interrogators and those who were experienced and talented in this field had to create strict protocols for interviews that were often carried out by others. These involved a series of meticulously prepared plans to assist trainee interrogators, which indicated the type of vocabulary required for that particular interrogation, the rank of the prisoner, and his background and military experience. With training in and increasing familiarity with

14 Arthur Page, *Between Victor and Vanquished—An Australian Interrogator in the War against Japan*, Australian Military History Unit, Loftus, 2008.

Japanese military language and nuances, interrogators were often able to develop close relationships with their subject. Japanese prisoners were astonished to find that Australians could speak Japanese, let alone be familiar with the precise military language of the Japanese military forces. Page found that most Japanese prisoners quickly became cooperative due to the shock and anxiety of capture and the surprise at being offered simple kindness by their captors. As a result, there were few problems when interrogating the Japanese prisoners.

As with any group, there were some individuals who proved to be obstinate and difficult. This was especially so with the officers and men of the Japanese Navy and Air Force who experienced the war in relative comfort compared to the soldiers who were abandoned, starving and diseased, in the New Guinea jungle. This discrepancy in wartime experience between the ordinary infantryman and the elite of the navy and air force was often exploited by their captors to unsettle a prisoner.

Page recalled an incident with a difficult and militant subject who revealed early on that he would not be providing any information to the Allies. The interrogation went non-stop for more than 30 hours. Violence or intimidation was never used—just simple and sustained questioning. The prisoner was allowed toilet breaks and to eat meals, but decided to stand for the whole time. Interrogators took turns in the room, patiently repeating questions. Eventually, it was time that wore him down. Through his own obstinacy he had lost the battle of wills, eventually breaking down and apologising to his captors for being 'such a cretin!'

Prisoners were initially classified as likely to have information of a particular type or value and these details accompanied them in the meticulously kept records that followed them through their various situations to higher levels of interrogation. Many prisoners were only processed in a rudimentary way, but others had their files marked to indicate they may be able to provide particular insights into specific military areas. All Japanese prisoners had a designation 'PWJA' ('A' for 'Australia') followed by a six-digit number. Some prisoners were also designated 'PWJA (USA)' to indicate they were under American control. Fanatical and hardline Italian fascists had an 'X' on their designations; for example, 'PWIX 123456'. The 'X' was a handy identifier for the prisoner as they moved through the system, indicating that the prisoner was a 'difficult one'. While Naka and other Japanese were recognised early on as falling into that category, the Allies did not use the X classification on Japanese prisoners. Naka, at least, was initially reasonably compliant. Torn by his sense of guilt and culpability over the men of his platoon and his 'surrender', it was some months later that he became a problem for the Allies.

One prisoner in particular became a particular focus for the Allies during his internment in Brisbane. While nearly all Japanese were eventually processed and transferred to Cowra, this particular prisoner was kept longer and became of great interest to ATIS. It was discovered that he possessed an extraordinary memory and during his time of imprisonment from 1943–45 he revealed the Japanese Military Code almost in its entirety. Australia may not have had an Alan Turing who cracked the Enigma Code, but we did have this brilliant individual. As a result of his invaluable assistance to the Allies, he was feted and even occasionally taken into Brisbane to see the movies while dressed in an Allied uniform!

Prisoners were also assessed by their interrogator and given a rating according to their intelligence value: 'A' signified that the prisoner's information was assessed as completely reliable; 'B' usually reliable; 'C' fairly reliable; 'D' not usually reliable; and 'E' unreliable. An 'F' classification indicated that the truth of the information from the prisoner could not be accurately ascertained. Interrogation usually commenced with an attempt to put the prisoner at ease. This normally involved informal greeting and a casual chat about the prisoner's health, the weather, and other incidentals such as: 'Are you being well looked after under the circumstances?' These casual discussions were designed to get the prisoner to drop their guard and to relax. Page witnessed many instances where a newly captured prisoner was in such a state of anxiety that any interrogation was almost impossible.

* * *

Page's job in these circumstances was to re-establish a more laidback ambience with a series of innocuous questions concerning the prisoner's home and domestic circumstances and the offer of a cigarette or sweet. Combining the giving of small gifts and showing compassion for the prisoner's circumstances with an absence of stress or urgency in the language and speech of the interrogator almost invariably successfully reduced the prisoner's anxiety levels. A number of Japanese prisoners confirmed after the war that they had felt an obligation to be helpful to their interrogators because of how well they had been treated.

Australia and the USA generally only used one interrogator per prisoner whereas the British system involved the use of two. The Australians had observed the impact of using two people but decided that prisoners who were already in a general state of confusion would be less likely to provide the information required to two people than to one. Australian interrogators decided early on in the war to take a softly-softly approach to prisoners and they only resorted to harsh language or threats when absolutely necessary. The use of sweets and other sugar treats as a reward and inducement was important to the process as the Japanese have a penchant for candy and most had undergone extreme privations before capture. The simple question 'When was the last time you tasted sugar?' used by the interrogators was surprisingly effective, with one prisoner breaking down when offered a sweet; such were the terrible conditions experienced by the Japanese soldiers in the jungle. Many interrogators felt genuine sympathy for the Japanese and the terrible hardships they had faced. When captured, Japanese soldiers were bedraggled, dirty, unshaven, starving and their uniforms were in rags; they were so desperate that they would often plead with their captors to kill them. Most were also confused and in a turbulent state of mind having never envisaged being a captive. The idea was simply beyond their understanding and, yet, here they were, a prisoner of the Allies. They had been taught to commit suicide immediately upon knowing a battle was lost; but had not done so. Almost invariably they showed no capability, intention or interest in escaping; they simply did not know how to do it. They were alone without their 'family' of corporals, sergeants and officers. In the meantime, the interrogator's job was to capitalise on this opportunity and to milk the prisoners of all worthwhile information.

The typical opening conversation from the interrogator, who held all the aces in this game of strategy and psychology, was designed to play with the mind of the anxious and vulnerable prisoner. The questioner would start by observing that the prisoner might have expected to be killed or at least bashed, like his sergeant used to do in training. 'We do not do that, because you are worth more than that,' the interrogator would say. The interrogator would stress that the problem with the Japanese soldiers was that they did not know when to stop fighting because they were afraid to surrender.

The questioner would then state that the Allies do not kill people for fun in a barbaric way, like the Japanese. A series of statements would be made to ground the prisoner in his situation. He would be told that such behaviour was an extremely serious war crime, and killing himself would not help him or his family. He had fought well but now it was over. As a prisoner, he had a duty to end this war, just as the Allies did; he was being treated well and was safe, so he should try to behave with gratitude. One day he would be going back to his country to restore the nation. Wasn't that a better view of things than his indoctrination?

During this set speech, cigarettes and other comforts were usually offered to the prisoner. In most cases, this 'good cop' approach worked and the subsequent cooperation resulted in information being handed over quite freely. Other prisoners, though, would try and 'weave a story' without realising that the interrogator always had the upper hand with current information on all the Japanese units that were fighting. When confronted with lying, which was against the military code of the Japanese Army, prisoners would often turn bright red with embarrassment and, knowing that they had been caught out, would apologise profusely and then freely reveal all that they knew.

There were some difficult and cunning prisoners who would attempt to lie and then simply keep going. Page remembered one situation where a prisoner proceeded with his story for more than five minutes while, at the same time, Page could barely keep a straight face because he knew full well that the prisoner was lying. In these instances, the interrogator would spring his trap using what he knew to be the truth about a particular situation. Accusing the prisoner of lying would usually lead to a swift and profound confession. Another tactic was to question a prisoner one day, let him go and bring him back the next day, when his lie would be revealed in front of him. Being a convincing liar required excellent recall and, unfortunately for the majority of prisoners, that was not their strong suit. They often had difficulty in remembering the details and their story ultimately fell apart. There was one lie that many did end up keeping and that was their false name, presumably to avoid their family knowing of their capture.

* * *

Another ATIS interrogator was the remarkable and jovial Alister Kentwell whose background was similar to that of Page.[15] He would see service as an interrogator in both Australia and Borneo. Kentwell was born in 1925 in Kobe, Japan, the son of a Japanese-born mother with Danish and Swedish heritage and an Australian father. He later recalled fond memories of growing up in Japan and attending the Canadian Academy School where he met children from all over the world, including Jewish children, many of whom had left Germany with their parents due to the Nazis.

Arriving in Australia at the age of 13 with his parents, one of his first impressions of Australia was that of a quite intolerant country. He had spent his childhood growing up with children from all over the world yet, here, he felt isolated in a largely white Anglo-Celtic society. It was a wonderful country, but different in its attitudes to foreigners. He spent five years at school in Brisbane until he was called up and sent to the No. 3 Army Recruit Training Battalion at the Military Training Camp at Cowra. His future involvement with the army had

15 The author interviewed Alister in February 2016. His World War II experience later led him to university, back to Japan to teach and a distinguished career in the Australian Department of Foreign Affairs and Trade working in Japan, South Korea and Malaysia.

been pre-destined through his parents' contacts with the family of Captain George Charlesworth. After completing three months' basic training, he was sent to the Hume Army Camp near Albury. It was what was termed a 'holding camp' and he was unsure why he had been sent there. A little later he was transferred to Brisbane to the ATIS centre at Gaythorne. Upon his arrival in an American Army bus (there were no army trucks for the interrogators!) he was met by the man who would become his mentor, Lieutenant Reuben Mann, who gave him a thorough orientation of the ATIS facility. Mann became a confidant and warned him of various individuals within the organisation.[16]

Kentwell, along with others at the centre, was required to demonstrate his linguistic proficiency. With his background and fluency in Japanese, however, this was easily achieved. He was just 18 years old when he started this vital work. The sharp-eyed Captain George Charlesworth personally selected the first prisoner who he thought Kentwell would be able to interrogate successfully. Because he was first a corporal and later a sergeant, Kentwell generally only interrogated Japanese prisoners with an equivalent rank or below that of officer level; unless there was a special case. Although fluent in Japanese, he was not familiar with the Japanese military terminology and had to learn quickly by sitting in with experienced men to pick up terms for the units, tactics, weapons and organisational structure of the Imperial Japanese Army.

His interrogations were based entirely at Gaythorne and not at the other centre at Indooroopilly and were usually held under canvas on duckboard floors. There was an armed guard inside and Kentwell had to take his own notes. When interviewed in 2016 about his work, Kentwell said that he and other interrogators were not considered interpreters of information but simply information-gatherers. He said that they were constantly being exhorted by ATIS to: 'just get information, just get information'.

When each prisoner was brought in for interrogation, there was a chair in front of the interrogator's desk and almost all prisoners

16 Mann, to be known as Captain "Poppa" Mann would be transffered to Cowra.

sat down. Kentwell offered them a cigarette and then told them to keep the packet, as a gesture of goodwill which was much appreciated by the prisoner. Most internees were Japanese but he did run across the occasional Korean who spoke Japanese and was serving with the Japanese Army. Kentwell said that he always referred to these as 'Korean gentlemen', a joke title which they appreciated and which generally encouraged the release of information. A typical interrogation would run for two spells, usually on the morning and afternoon of the same day. Early on in the life of ATIS, a third morning session would be added if further information was required or needed checking. Prisoners started to object to this third session and the interrogators were instructed, wherever possible, to complete their work in a maximum of two sessions. A pro-forma document was provided for each prisoner with the first task being to fill out all personal details of the prisoner—when they enlisted, where they went, what the names of the ships were—before they tried to get the serious information.

Kentwell was later effusive in describing how the Japanese reacted under interrogation. 'They loved it … they just wanted to talk and tell everything they knew!' He believed that the Japanese saw no future for themselves in Japan and so were resigned to never returning. Seemingly there was no conflict in their minds about handing over any military information that they had.

Kentwell agreed that the prisoners knew that giving up this information betrayed their fellow soldiers; nevertheless, they had been forced to deal with their own particular situation. Kentwell knew that he needed to probe the prisoners' thoughts at times and was interested in what they thought about returning to Japan. 'When I spoke to a prisoner and referred to Japan, I did not use "Nippon" but rather "Naichi" which is "homeland". This had a profound and different effect on them.' While interrogations were always conducted in a calm and courteous way with the interrogator working to gain the prisoner's confidence, Kentwell did not personally find the prisoners likeable. There was one exception to this general observation with a relationship he described as 'truly friendly'.

When interviewed in 2016, two interrogations stood out in his memory. One prisoner was a sleepy, nondescript type who didn't seem to care about anything until Kentwell discovered that he was a Zero pilot. After this, he couldn't keep the pilot quiet; he spent all his time talking about the new Zero Model 52 Zeke. Kentwell was excited and thought he had hit an intelligence goldmine, but when he reported this to ATIS he was advised: 'No … we know all about the Zeke … keep going for other stuff.'

The second memorable prisoner revealed that he was a member of the Black Dragon Society. This powerful group was created at the start of the 20th century, mainly for espionage on the Manchurian, Russian and Siberian borders. Other activities developed over time and its membership extended to senior military personnel and even Japanese Cabinet mini7ters. This exotic group appeared to be an oriental assortment of spies with its members adhering to various nationalistic principles.[17]

Kentwell made some personal observations on Japanese prisoners. He noticed that once they had settled down after the initial trauma of capture, they were generally well-balanced individuals. The anxiety and guilt that they had initially felt dissipated with the reality of their confinement and their enjoyment of the excellent conditions provided for them. He offered the opinion that, considering his experience at that time and with all the Japanese he had seen, Lieutenant Maseo Naka's associated guilt at having lost all his men was not typical.

17 The Black Dragon Gang emerged later at the Cowra camp in 1946 amongst Chinese prisoners attached to Japanese forces and was responsible for a number of murders and assaults inside their compound.

CHAPTER 7
NAKA'S INTERROGATION

Naka had, up to this point, maintained that his name was Hideo Yamashita but the deception was about to be undone. He had been interrogated once and was now to face his second session because the Australian officer in charge of his case was convinced he had not been truthful. Interrogators knew that prisoners would try and deceive and they used techniques to ensure that, wherever possible, prisoners' statements were verified and validated. A number of things about Naka did not add up and the interrogation was about to take a new direction. The first session had been relatively 'soft' but now pressure would be applied. Hideo Yamashita, as he was then known, was advised that an Australian officer would be speaking with him the next day and that an escort of guards would take him to the captain's tent which had been allocated for the day. He was to have his breakfast and be ready. The guards duly arrived at 7.30 am and escorted him through walkways to the tent—the same journey as before. Naka was nervous and wary and kept looking around. He saw no other Japanese there and knew he was alone. The guard, a corporal, ushered him inside, through the open tent flaps where the officer was seated at a small desk. As Naka entered, the officer did not stand, but looked up and nodded to the guard who turned and stationed himself outside.

Speaking in excellent Japanese but with a European accent, the captain once again offered Naka a chair. The previous day the Australian had smiled but not this day. Naka sat down; his shoulders were slumped and his eyes were focused on the dust that lay on the duckboard floor. He knew he was in trouble. There were no cigarettes on the table this time. The conversation, based on original records, proceeded in Japanese:

'Yesterday you told me you were from Kyushu but a little later that you were born in Hiroshima ... where?'

'I am from Kyushu but enlisted near Hiroshima.'

'You said you sailed from Japan straight to New Britain but you boasted about overcoming the allies at Singapore. Where did you serve?'

Naka shrugged.

'You said you never fought against the Australians at Kokoda but we know your unit was there ... wasn't it?'

No answer.

'You are an officer in the Imperial Japanese Army ... have you no respect? Do you tell lies to superiors all the time ... aren't you ashamed?'

Naka then danced around all these subjects and fell exactly where the interrogator wanted. He was confused and in an instant he broke.

'My name is Naka Maseo ... I am not Yamashita.'[18]

'Why did you lie to us?'

'I do not want to say.'

'Are being treated well?'

'Yes, I am.'

'You would probably prefer a Japanese futon ... but is your bed comfortable?'

Naka may well have thought of his mother preparing his rollout mattress when he was a child. He nodded a 'yes'.

'And the food is it to your liking?'

'Yes, it is satisfactory. The fish is fresh but the rice is not the same.'

'Yes, we know ... it is not sticky the way Japanese like it.'

Again, another nod to say that he agreed.

'Have you had the medical treatment you require?'

'Yes ... for malaria and scabies.'

'So why are you not a grateful and honourable Japanese officer?'

Naka sat bolt upright.

---

18 Japanese people will nearly always use their family name first followed by their given name.

'I formally request as an honourable Japanese officer that I be provided with a pistol so that I may commit suicide!'

The captain refrained from reacting to this demand.

'That is plainly ridiculous ... why do you want to die?'

'I cannot return to Japan because, as an officer, it is my duty to die.'

Naka, emotional, gushed forth a protracted speech where he admitted that his death would benefit neither his country nor his comrades but it was something that he had to do; he had no other option. He said that either he would kill himself in Australia or he would be executed upon his return to Japan.

'No, your request will not be granted.'

'Then I request to be shot.'

'Again, no ... you request is refused and, Lieutenant Naka, I require that you answer my questions.'

Naka again dropped his head. He had lost any power that he thought he had in the situation and now had nothing left, nothing except information.

The captain commenced with the basics: confirming where he grew up, where he went to school, his employment before the war and when he was conscripted. He had been selected for officer training but before that had gone through the ranks, being promoted to corporal, sergeant and sergeant major over a period of just eight months. Naka revealed great detail about the Japanese operations and this information was matched with what the Allies already knew about his unit; its operations in Malaya, the Philippines and in New Guinea where the Allies' current engagement was the principal area of interest.

After the Philippines, Naka sailed for Rabaul in New Britain and then on to New Guinea to join in the fighting at Kokoda. He recounted the great difficulties experienced by the Japanese troops who were given few provisions and these only sufficient for a fortnight.

'How were you expected to live?'

'We Japanese soldiers were expected to live off the land or capture the Allies' food stores. When food was short my men's morale plummeted ... horsemeat was a luxury when we could get it.'

'As a lieutenant you were a platoon commander?'

'Yes.'

'So what was the structure of your platoon; what weapons did you have?'

'Just after we landed in New Guinea my platoon had two rifle sections, each with standard-issue rifles, the 38 in 6.5 mm and a Taisho 11 light machine gun and one grenade discharger section.'

'Were these effective?'

'The light machine gun was a good weapon but it used a lot of ammunition but we always had plenty. The grenade discharger (light mortar) section had two dischargers. I did not like this weapon because it could not be used with overhead vegetation and had a small effective burst area.'

'What communications did you have and what type of radios?'

'No, we never had radios. Our field and communications were by runners which depleted the fighting strength of forward units.'

'So messages were written?'

'Never … only verbal commands.'

'We can arrange for you to write home to your mother.'

'No, no, she will already know that I am dead: Killed in Action.'

Naka stoically told his interrogator that because of his 'death' his mother would receive a one-off monetary offering.[19] The captain recognised Naka's vulnerability at this point, produced a packet of cigarettes and matches and placed them on Naka's side of the table. Naka fumbled to get one out of the packet and pushed it back across the desk.

'No … keep them' and then the information flowed like a river.

Naka was not worried about his mother as he believed that his brother would look after her. He said that he did not believe in the war but, as a conscript and a loyal Japanese, he was simply doing his duty. He did not think that Tojo, the Japanese Prime Minister, was responsible and he thought that the decision to enter the war must have been considered carefully as the emperor would not have allowed his people to be plunged into a conflict so needlessly. Naka thought

19 Around $US25,000 in today's equivalent.

that, in general, Japan would have been happier keeping out of the war but had little choice in the matter. He had read a Japanese version of Hitler's *Mein Kampf* (My Struggle) but felt that the Japanese people did not accept the Nazi notion of racial superiority. The section of the book which had stuck in his mind was the statement that: 'an amicable treaty with a country was a valuable prelude to an attack on that country.' He felt strongly that Hitler had made a 'cat's paw' (a person manipulated to serve the interests of another), out of Japan. Naka and his men thought that, after their combat service in China, Malaya and the Philippines, their unit would be sent home. They were clearly not happy about being sent to New Guinea. He said he knew that there were Japanese and Korean 'comfort women' supplied in various types of brothels for the soldiers and that some men contracted venereal diseases, but they appeared to recover after treatment.

Naka's fighting experience in three theatres of war had been quite different. In China there had been some sharp clashes but they were soon resolved. In Malaya, it was much more difficult but ultimately successful. New Guinea, on the other hand, had been a test of endurance under trying conditions and his unit had suffered greatly from sickness and inadequate supplies. Casualties were around 50 per cent, mostly from sickness. Medical support was a constant problem for the Japanese, especially as every man in his unit had malaria. He said that he had not heard of cannibalism taking place but told his interrogators that, under the extremely difficult circumstances that the Japanese found themselves, he would not have been surprised if it had occurred. He said that Japanese soldiers had been told to respect foreign peoples whose countries they had invaded but, because the conditions had become so stressful in wartime, those ideals had fallen by the wayside.

His interrogation was completed on 23 March 1943 and he returned to the Gaythorne camp.

His persistent desire to take his own life continued and on 28 March at 11 am he requested that a sentry shoot him: 'Shoot me: give me that gun … I'll not shoot you.' Naka was then locked in a cell for his own safety. The next day when he was interviewed and asked why he wanted to commit suicide he simply stated that, as all his men had been shot, he wished to join them and that he had no fear of death. He said that it was the Japanese rule that an officer must join his men. Two days later, on 30 March, he had taken no food and was on a hunger strike. It was decided to place him in isolation and under constant surveillance. This also had the effect of limiting his influence on other prisoners who may have become aware of his protests.

It was this troubled soul, with his mixture of honour and defiance, pride and pity, who would soon be transferred to Cowra Prisoner of War Camp. It would be there that he would make his indelible mark on the military history of both Australia and Japan.

CHAPTER 8
BUILD MORE CAMPS

Australia's prisoner of war camp system during Wold War II developed largely from its involvement in World War I, 25 years earlier. In spite of that experience, the internment processes and prisoner of war administration were initially slow to react to the declaration of war against Germany. Under British command in North Africa a portion of the large numbers of mainly Italian prisoners captured there would eventually be allocated to Australia. A little later, the system then had to adjust to the speedy entry into the war of Japan with the initial internment of Japanese civilians from Australia and surrounding areas. Later it would be Japanese military personnel. The system of administration and operation that was required was necessarily complex and vast. It ultimately became the subject of a highly detailed postwar report by the Australian Directorate of Prisoners of War and Internees.

In 1939 there were no military prisoners of war in Australia at all, but there were a number of native-born German and Italians who called this country home. Added to this was a group of other nationalities in Australia from countries which had become part of the Axis powers headed by Germany. This group, oddly enough, included a small group of Muslim immigrants from pre-war Albania. Italy had invaded Albania and overtaken the government and this event, by the unforgiving standards of the times, placed the local Albanians in the Axis camp. Even though many of these mainly German and Italian men, women and children had been in Australia for a number of years, and even generations, and were to all practical purposes citizens, they were systematically rounded up and interned. As well as imprisoning these mostly innocent residents, there was also a genuine requirement to locate and detain Nazi sympathisers—those who had quite publically announced their support for Hitler prior to September 1939. It is easy to forget that, prior to the declaration of war, there were large sections of people in many Western countries sympathetic and even supportive of the fascists. Therefore, this was a system developed to arrest, isolate and intern potential spies and saboteurs and also to prevent civilian and military personnel from contributing to the enemy's war effort. It is important to remember that Australia took its obligations under the Geneva Convention very seriously and increasingly so as the war progressed. At war's end, Australia could reflect on the fact that its treatment of prisoners of war and internees met, and in many cases exceeded, the required standards of the Geneva Convention. Nevertheless, the administration and operation of these prisoner of war camps was far from perfect.

Understanding the operation of Cowra Prisoner of War Camp in context requires an examination of the many other such camps in Australia that operated from 1939 through to 1947. Prisoners of war kept that designation even after war's end and while some rules were relaxed they were still under guard until shipping became available to return them to their homelands. Furthermore, we need to see the operation of the camp through the framework of Australia at war, perceiving itself to be in a desperate fight for survival, and how the system of interning enemy combatants changed and adapted after Japan's entry into the war in 1941. The Japanese threat was well recognised and the War Cabinet had decided, as early as June 1940, upon a policy of interning any Japanese in Australia and its territories in the event of war.

When Prime Minister Robert Menzies unilaterally announced in September 1939 that, as a consequence of Britain declaring war on Germany, so too had Australia, an administrative process was set in train that would eventually see a large number of camps and lower-grade internment facilities built and systematically managed. Initially, National Security Regulations had to be established that defined, interpreted and implemented the agreed terms of the Geneva Convention that Australia had both ratified and signed for the treatment of prisoners of war. These regulations established uniform and comprehensive policies from which the actions of our soldiers, guards and camp administrators could be authorised. While the requirements of the Geneva Convention were seemingly inflexible and even pedantic, the Australian Government considered this to be the only acceptable and appropriate foundation for the treatment and internment of enemy soldiers.

While the 21st-century 'War on Terror' highlights how security regulations are always a balancing act between individual freedoms and public safety and can be subject to adverse media and public comment, the adherence to the Geneva Convention by Australia provided a safeguard against criticism which waxed and waned according to the war's progress. This strict observance of the convention also became a convenient defence for the government when criticised over its treatment of internees. In most cases when queried, the minister would simply announce that the actions taken were requirements of the convention.

This meant that enemy captives, particularly civilian internees, had their rights administered and overseen by the 'Protecting Power' under the Convention—in this case representatives of the Swiss Government in Australia. The enemy's privileges under the convention were often accomplished with great reluctance, but in general they were generally strictly adhered to, in many cases to a higher standard than was required. Designed as a reciprocal arrangement for warring nations, Australia's management of internees became less contentious when the treatment of Australian prisoners, particularly by the Japanese, became widely known.

Throughout the war, the administration of the provisions of the Geneva Convention by the Directorate of Prisoners of War and Internees was conducted with firmness and fairness. Bitter experience from World War I showed that our enemies were inclined to mirror any perceived ill-treatment of their captured soldiers by visiting similar or worse retribution on Allied prisoners of war. This concern increased following the loss of the 8th Division and other Australian units to the Japanese forces after the fall of Singapore in February 1942.

The responsibility to enforce and adhere to these obligations during World War II was assigned to Australia for any prisoners captured by

Australian forces. It also applied to those held in the Commonwealth on behalf of the governments of the United Kingdom and, later, the United States. In the early part of the war this was not a major problem as the principal security concerns lay with the 'enemy within', and the directorate was mainly responsible for all enemy 'aliens' resident in Australia and other territories under its control. As the war progressed, a separate administrative arm was established to handle prisoners, both German and Italian, from the North African and Middle East campaigns.

Despite common misconceptions, internment of civilians was only used when other methods of 'control' were believed to be ineffective. Of most interest to the authorities were enemy aliens (ethnic groups) resident in Australia with young men of military service age. These young men were believed to be more prone to 'take up arms' for their countries of origin or affinity and were therefore immediate candidates for internment. While some leeway was allowed to former residents and descendants from the European Axis powers and their 'nationals', circumstances were far different after Japan entered the war. Japanese internments commenced immediately after the 8 December 1941 attack on Pearl Harbor (being on the western side of the International Date Line, 8 December in Australia was 7 December in Hawaii).

By January 1942, only weeks after Japan's entry into the war, about 1100 Japanese residents were interned in Australia, with another 3180 Japanese transferred from overseas locations for internment here. These mostly innocent victims of war— farmers, merchants and pearl divers—were forcibly relocated from areas under Allied control, including Iran, Palestine, Indonesia, New Caledonia, New Hebrides, Solomon Islands, New Zealand and other South Pacific locations.

Other internees were also accepted under an arrangement with Great Britain, and the tragic story of the ship HMT *Dunera* and the treatment of its mostly refugee passengers fleeing Nazism has been recounted many times. Other unusual groups transported to Australia as internees included Indonesian Communists fighting the Dutch colonial powers and a small number of French Foreign Legionnaires who had deserted in Indochina but had subsequently been assessed as a security risk. Because of the capacity issues in the system, many of the internees were initially held in civilian gaols awaiting the building of a number of internment camps, which included the one at Cowra.

A little known prisoner exchange also took place in August 1942 following protracted negotiations between the United Kingdom and Japan. An exchange of civilians between Japan and Australia was subsequently agreed with the *City of Canterbury* leaving Melbourne on 8 August with 34 Japanese officials, 533 Japanese internees and four Siamese (Thai) nationals sailing to Lourenco Marques (now Maputo), the capital of Mozambique in Africa. Seventy-seven Australian military personnel were also present on the ship. In exchange, a party of 30 Australians, 71 British nationals, 14 Dutch and miscellaneous other nationalities were returned to Australia.

Australia's first significant military commitment in World War II was fighting with British forces against the Axis powers in North Africa. In these actions, large numbers of Italian prisoners were captured. Although strategically advantageous, this gave Britain a huge logistical problem. Camps for the Italian prisoners were initially constructed in North Africa and then India, but disease and food shortages saw Britain approach the Australian Government asking it to provide additional prisoner accommodation. Australia initially agreed to take 50,000 Italians, though this request was later reduced to 12,000 due to the limited numbers of ships available to transport these prisoners. The final arrangement meant that the construction of the camps in Australia would be at British expense with a further seven shillings a day cost for housing and maintaining each prisoner. The numbers of Italian prisoners in Australia would eventually reach a total of 15,000. When Australia began to take Japanese prisoners on behalf of the United States, it was also agreed that these would be the financial responsibility of America, again at seven shillings a day. The USA did not pay this amount as it was absorbed into the 'Reverse Lend Lease' program that required Australia to fund much of the Americans' military and logistical requirements while in Australia.

CHAPTER 8

The sudden increase in the numbers of prisoners Australia had to accommodate required estimates to be made of potential totals and the resources needed to quarter them. Based on these figures, the Australian Government decided that it was necessary for three prisoner of war camps to be constructed in New South Wales, with one of these to be built at Cowra. The decision to recommend Cowra, due to its location and relative isolation, was telephoned to the army's Director General of Engineering Services (DGES) at 1.30 pm on Saturday, 3 May 1941. The Director General agreed with the selection and immediately proceeded to make it a reality. The next step was to select the actual site for the camp with cost a most definite consideration. On Sunday, 4 May, only a day after the decision had been made, Major John Connan left Sydney by car in the company of Lieutenant Egan and a Mr Doyle, a surveyor. They inspected four potential sites on the outskirts of Cowra and immediately made their selection. They met with the local government authorities and contractors and stressed the urgency and short time frame of the project.

While cost was always a factor, it was decided that a camp for up to 4,000 prisoners of war, plus their guards, could simply not be serviced adequately by a septic sewage system, and so connection to the township's sewer system was considered a must. As soon as that construction had begun, an urgent problem arose. The new prisoner of war camp was being constructed in the 'danger zone' of the local rifle range, meaning that stray bullets could fly or fall at any time, which was not considered a great prospect for the contractors, guards and, later, prisoners on the site. In the time-honoured tradition of the defence forces, much argument then arose between the 'prisoner of war camp faction' and the 'rifle-range faction' within the army, with each insisting that the other must give way! When the bickering was over, it was finally agreed that a rifle range was still required in Cowra with a new facility developed 9 miles (13 km) out of town, at the quaintly named location of 'Whistle Waa'.

After a number of considerable difficulties, the necessities of war came into play and from March to June 1941, a supreme effort was made by the army and its contractors to ensure that the camp was functioning, in a rudimentary way, by June of that year. Its first occupants would be the garrison soldiers and the mainly Italian civilian internees that they guarded.

The government now had to appoint an 'Official Visitor' as per the Geneva Convention and in line with the policy it had adopted for prisoner of war camps in World War I. It was agreed that the internees should have their 'condition of internment' reviewed by civilians, that they should be afforded some assistance owing to their sudden removal from civil life, that 'reasonable standards' of accommodation should be provided to them to minimise retaliation by the Axis powers, and that regular inspections should be carried out and duly recorded to defend against unfounded complaints. Cowra's Official Visitor was the esteemed judge The Honourable Sir Frederick Jordan, Chief Justice of NSW. In addition to the Australian visitor, there was also required a 'Protecting Power' for the enemy interns, with the Swiss Consulate in Sydney appointed to act in this role as a neutral power. The Swiss were to play a more prominent and forceful role in monitoring military prisoners as they began to arrive in increasing numbers. Being mindful of its own prisoners in Axis hands, Australia always dutifully and scrupulously operated under the conditions of the Geneva Convention. Interestingly, there was often a cat-and-mouse game played with the Swiss who took a punctilious and unbending view of their responsibilities. The internees at Cowra, though, were not there for long and, except for the notable case of Japanese civilians, most of those interned in Australia were subsequently released back into the community within nine to 12 months, after security checks revealed their non-existent or minimal threat to 'the war effort'.

Generally, the internees caused little trouble from a security point of view at Cowra. There were some isolated incidents at other camps including the murder of one Italian internee by another, and the discovery of a tunnel at the Loveday camp which had all but been completed and was ready for the tunnelers to escape. This was comprised of a group of Germans from Iran which included a number of known

Nazi sympathisers. That the tunnel was discovered was fortunate as it was believed that this group was planning either sabotage or some other mayhem once outside the confines of the barbed wire.

The personal experiences of many of these internees, mostly ordinary individuals, was no doubt traumatic and unpleasant, especially for those whose families and businesses had made Australia home for decades. One such group that ultimately escaped internment were a party of Jewish refugees who had escaped from Germany to Australia before the invasion of Poland. Unfortunately, the group still had German passports and, upon arrival, the first impulse of the Australian authorities was to lock them all up! Common sense prevailed, however, after intense lobbying from Jewish groups in Australia who argued that these Jews could not be both Nazis and simultaneously targeted by the Nazis. When this logic was finally accepted, they were reclassified from 'Enemy Aliens' to 'Friendly Aliens'. A number of these individuals and families subsequently came to Cowra and established themselves on a farm on the outskirts of town.

* * *

Staffing and administration of the Cowra camp generally reflected the overall experience of camp operations throughout Australia. The major camps were the ones at Cowra and Hay in NSW, Tatura and Murchison in Victoria, and Loveday, South Australia, with many other smaller camps of varying security which included farms and hostels. Cowra also had a second camp which was known as the 'POW Camp Farm' some 8 km from the camp proper. This facility played an important role in growing food for the American-built cannery at Cowra producing rations for US and Australian troops as well as providing training for Italian prisoners who were transferred around NSW to work on private farms. There was also a little known third 'Cowra Camp' at Lae in New Guinea. This seemingly anomalous situation was the result of a deliberate strategy to ensure that transfers between Cowra and New Guinea did not have to be reported to the Swiss as these were strictly internal transfers within the 'same camp'!

Security was always of central importance at Cowra, followed by 'keeping the peace', which meant keeping the prisoners reasonably happy. This was achieved with the provision of materials for craft activities, musical instruments for entertainment, and work details, all overlaid with the required level of discipline. These were all designed to lower the anxiety levels that all internees suffered from, especially when first interned. Generally, security was viewed with an eye to the logistical practicalities of the camp. The report prepared after the breakout stated that: 'The task (of providing secure camps) was aggravated and quite rightly, that it was contrary to efficient prosecution of the war to require a state of security which would preclude all possibility of escape.' This, in essence, meant that, while all efforts would be made to deny prisoners the chance to escape, there was a limit to the resources available to achieve a perfectly secure facility.

Accordingly, due to these resource limitations, it was emphasised that the quality of the guards at these facilities should be the best available and 'imbued with the spirit of security', that is, able to match wits with the prisoners. Experience showed that the first allotment of guards assigned to Cowra was unsatisfactory with security adversely affected. This followed the quick realisation that many of the prisoners were highly intelligent and had plenty of leisure time in which to plan escapes. Therefore, the guards had to be up to the task of matching them in patience, cunning and resources. The staffing position improved somewhat in 1942 with orders issued for a review of all existing personnel and the immediate withdrawal of those guards considered to be unsatisfactory. From this point, maturity, intelligence and the willingness and ability to do the job were strong considerations in recruitment. It must be remembered that a number of these guards were returned soldiers from World War I who still bore both the mental and physical scars of that conflict. Even as staff recruitment improved, the postwar reports stated that the situation was never fully rectified, with some draft intakes even containing confirmed hardened criminals.

Apart from those who were transferred in as 'regular' soldiers for specialist tasks, prison camp guards were never the standard of trained combat soldiers, nor were they expected to be. After the war, in the boastful afterglow of victory, the guards were often 'reminded' of this by returned Australian Imperial Force (AIF) soldiers and even by former militia troops. This was an unfair slur as these guards did not choose to be untrained. What appealed to many of them was simply the pay. Having just come out of the Great Depression, steady paid work was an attractive proposition. Some of these men probably considered themselves old soldiers, tough old warriors from World War I, who also saw some romance in a return to service life; others likely felt the need to 'do their bit' because of their sons serving overseas. At the Cowra camp, it was not uncommon for men to turn up, essentially as civilians, change into army clothing and be given a rifle and the most rudimentary training. Weapons were in short supply as Australia, along with other Dominion nations had sent significant stocks of military rifles to Britain after the Dunkirk evacuation. If weapons' training was provided, it was basic, with some guards issued with pre-World War I .310 Martini Cadet single-shot rifles.

An intelligence corps section was maintained at each camp to help keep an eye on the prisoners and internees and ensure security. The directorate recognised some deficiencies in this vital area of information gathering, with officers told to 'pull their weight' by keeping dossiers and reporting all data likely to affect security. Intelligence corps officers often complained that the information flow was frequently only in one direction; from them to the directorate. One highly regarded intelligence officer Lionel Boorman, of whom we will hear more later, protested that it was often the case that they would send reports 'up the line' but never receive anything back. This failure to provide all-round communications on matters of crucial intelligence was to have fatal consequences.

CHAPTER 9
SEND HIM TO COWRA

Confused, conflicted and suicidal, Japanese soldier and now prisoner of war, Naka's interrogation was now complete. From being a minor celebrity at Gaythorne he became just another POW and destined for a long rail journey down Australia's east coast. After a short stay at Holsworthy detention cells in Sydney, he boarded a train on 2 April 1943 and was on his way to his new home at Cowra.

Train trips in the 1940s had legendary status and the Australian railways were highly organised. Not only was their operation critical to the economy and the nation's social structure but it played a vital role in the war effort. In spite of that plaudit they had another reputation—they were bureaucratic and had different gauge lines as well as operating procedures. The New South Wales system was considered to be the best, certainly by New South Welshmen! The downside was that rail travel outside of the Sydney metropolitan area was long, arduous and often uncomfortable.

Naka was taken from his cell at Holsworthy and loaded onto an army truck and driven to the Liverpool station. He and the other 29 Japanese POW were not travelling by regular passenger train but by a 'Military Special' and special it was. This train on this day was set up to transport 30 Japanese in two end platform carriages and a brake van which were pulled by a 32 class steam locomotive. Security was paramount so the trip would not travel through heavily populated Sydney and over the Blue Mountains where an escaped prisoner would be almost impossible to find, but by the southern line on flatter or more open country. Steam trains were thirsty and hungry beasts so there would be a number of required stops for water and coal along the way and passengers, in this case prisoners of war, had to be fed. This was supplied by way of sandwich packs in brown paper bags—thick slices of white bread and corned beef from the railway refreshment rooms along the way. First stop on this long 10-hour journey was Goulburn for coal and water where the locomotive and firemen (coal shovellers) crew from Sydney changed and the Goulburn crew took over on the next leg of the run.

At the end of each carriage two guards kept constant watch on their captives. A stop for water or coal represented a potential security risk; however, as these special carriages had bars on each window the only possibility for an escape was from the ends of the carriages. Toilet cubicles were in the centre of each carriage and using the facility required a guard escort. These men were usually regular soldiers or military police and of a higher standard than POW camp guards. Their vigilance and physical presence were enough to dissuade any individual of an attempt to break loose. Should one have escaped, they were likely to be shot; however, during World War II no attempts were made. After Goulburn, more water was taken on at Fish River and further on at Harden and the locomotive was changed as the train was now moving into a new zone and locomotives only operated within their own areas. Finally the shipment of Japanese arrived at Cowra, 200 miles (312 km) west of Sydney, a rich agricultural but geographically isolated district with a hot Mediterranean climate.

The 30 Japanese prisoners who disgorged, tired and disoriented from that morning train at Cowra Railway Station, must have felt that they had been delivered to the ends of the earth. This sense of separation from the world was reinforced when they were herded into metal cages that had been constructed on the back of army trucks which then headed off through the town.

Naka had even more to worry about than his own internal conflicts. A bullying guard enjoying his meagre power to intimidate, told him: 'Be careful Nip when you get to the camp. They might do the same thing to you that they just did to the Japs in New Zealand!' This crude boast was in reference to an incident at Featherston Prisoner of War Camp on New Zealand's north island just six weeks earlier, where 48 Japanese prisoners from the Battle of Guadalcanal were shot dead by guards after rioting. Naka had already heard rumours of this event but these malicious comments confirmed his conviction that, sooner or later, he would be killed by the Australians.

This spectacle of Japanese prisoners being transported like livestock through the town often incited a chase by jeering children. Two months earlier similar groups had been pelted with leftovers from the local tomato crop, such was the antipathy towards the Japanese from many Australians at the time. Conversely, if the trucks had friendly Italian POW on board, the town's children would run behind hoping for a sweet or a handmade toy to be thrown out the back. Pretty teenage girls were often presented with a posy of flowers but none of those niceties came from the Japanese. The tomatoes had long gone so it was just 'cat-calling' that morning. While somewhat embarrassed at their antics 70 years ago, some local residents of Cowra can still recall the 'fun' that they had during these very public prisoner transfers.

The trucks rattled through the town some 3 miles (5 km) north of the central business district and continued onto a dusty unsealed road to the officially designated Prisoner of War and Internment Group No. 12. The 'Group' was in fact five distinct areas: four individual compounds, which were under the control of a company of around 100 guards. These were independently administered areas and at the time referred to as 'camps'. Above this area and overseeing the whole operation was the Garrison Headquarters with its commandant, 53-year-old Lieutenant Colonel Montague Ambrose 'Monty' Brown. Shielded from the harsh western sun below the crest of a granite outcropped hill, 30 office buildings, mess huts and sleeping quarters of black corrugated iron with asbestos roofs contained the staff with overall supervision and control of prisoner of war compounds A,B,C and D. All the guards at the PW and I Group were troops of the 22nd Garrison combined with the comings and goings of personnel from Australian and Allied units. Many of the guards were experienced soldiers, some less so and a number were of barely average quality.

Cowra was already a military town with a major recruit training facility on its outskirts to the south-east. The community was prospering from the many young soldiers (those over 21 who could legally drink) and instructors spending their relatively low pay at the local hotels and many dances held during the week. As well as the POW and military training camps there was a power alcohol factory producing 2.75 million gallons (12 million litres) of petrol each year and an annex of the Lithgow Small Arms factory. On the outskirts of town towards Gooloogong Jewish families from Germany and Austria had established a commune-farm. The town had matured considerably and was capitalising on the largesse of wages and supplies needed to feed the many troops and factory workers. The Edgells Cannery was under construction to produce food for the Allies and in December that year its one millionth can would roll off the production line. Additional housing was constructed in the 'duration' style, being plain and simple two-bedroom fibro cottages. The debt for the newly built St Raphaels Catholic Church was being speedily reduced from the proceeds of the regular dances run in its hall for the benefit of the troops. Vaudeville-style entertainment and local cinemas were regularly attended and often sold out. Dance partners were in high demand and became a problem in that local employers were complaining that their 'girls ' were so tired from their terpsichorean efforts that they were falling asleep at their daytime jobs! The local Chamber of Commerce had travelled to Sydney to request, and even demand in some cases, that the breweries who controlled hotels in those days upgrade their accommodation for the expected arrival of military personnel who would be living in town for the duration. Warrant and commissioned officers, often married, would be bringing their wives and sometimes children and would require something better that a 'pub room' over the main bar. Yes, all was going well, including two operating brothels in the town and a couple of freelancers known as Two-Ton Toni and Dirty Dora. The NSW Police Vice Squad paid regular visits to Cowra to keep an eye on what was recognised as a practical need where soldiers abound. The latter form of entertainment required the official establishment of a 'blue light depot' where soldiers were issued prophylactics before said entertainment (the term condoms would be used much later), or be treated afterwards, should the fun turn out otherwise.

The POW camp was bisected by a 780-metre-long access road ironically named 'Broadway' by the guards because of its intense floodlights and its whimsical resemblance to the theatre district of Broadway in New York. Broadway's southern gate provided access to both 'C' and 'D' compounds. After arriving at the camp, Naka and the others in his cage were ordered out of the truck and lined up, again under guard. He quickly surveyed the scene. To his left were around 30 to 35 buildings. These were well away from the 12-sided enclosure that was the secure area. He could see nothing of the town which he thought lay probably 1 to 2 km to the south-west and was shielded by rockstrewn hills. His first impression of the secure area was desolation. No trees existed, except in the distance well beyond the far perimeter, and all the ground had been cleared to bare dirt. The secure area was open ground but not flat and had a drop of around 30 metres from its highest to lowest point. The external fences were low, extremely low, around 1.5 metres. Were they electrified? No evidence of that could be seen. Inside this 12-sided area were around 150 buildings, with another 50-plus outside.

People came and went, some in civilian clothes, others in uniform. He could hear voices off to his right, not English, but yes, Italian. These men with dark hair and tanned skin pressed forward to look at him. They seemed happy and healthy and laughed, calling out to him something that sounded like 'Japoneesee'. Some of them ignored the show and chipped away at weeds in a garden. It was full of leafy vegetables and behind it were strange fountains and small structures like monuments. Were these prisoners of war, because if they were they did not act like it? A few of these men, dressed in the same cherry-coloured uniforms that Naka now had, were on the outside of the wire working alongside Australian soldiers. This was strange.

Some 300 metres away, in the middle of the area, were figures that looked familiar—by the way they walked and interacted with each other. They were Japanese and in a large group, maybe 500 or more. A few carried clubs—no, they were baseball bats—so they played baseball here.

Because of the perceived fanaticism of the Japanese prisoners, armed guards stood either side of the prisoners just outside the large wooden gates and barbed wire. Naka watched as the sergeants, corporals and privates from his group were separated and marched off to B Compound. Naka, as the only officer, was to be taken to D3 compound which was one of three sub-units in D Camp.

New Zealand-born Captain Leslie Eric Desmond Lees was the 'Officer of the Guard' on the day and he led the escort party up to the first gate. The procedure was a standard one; once inside there would be the traditional introduction of the new prisoner to the senior Japanese officer. Naka was about to enter a new world where a regimented system of limited activity and idleness would rule his daily life. It was a far cry from his wartime experiences as an officer in the elite 41st Infantry Regiment in China, Indochina, Malaya, Singapore and the Philippines, and its subsequent reversals in New Guinea. In contrast, this new routine promised him little to look forward to other than constant surveillance and the daily grind and immense boredom of prison life. While he may not have appreciated this at the time, it also offered safety, regular food, shelter, uninterrupted sleep, and access to medical facilities.

The entire D Camp area was separated into three separate areas known as 'D1' to 'D3'. The areas known as 'D1' and 'D2' held a range of national and political groups over the life of the camp from 1941 to 1947, from Indonesian internees to Italian fascists, Chinese and Koreans. 'D3' held the Japanese officers who, although not entitled to their own accommodation under the Geneva Convention, the authorities considered it a good idea to separate from the warrant officers, non-commissioned officers and other ranks. Lees had formally notified the Japanese officers' leader the day before of Naka's arrival. Arrangements were made for Naka's accommodation and the time for the official handover. Allied prisoners during the war were usually excited to welcome a new arrival as they brought news of the outside world and the progress of the war. The Japanese were similarly curious but became less enthusiastic as time went on as increasing numbers of prisoners arriving showed that their forces were beginning to suffer.

The Japanese at this stage were still considered by the public to be winning the war, despite the major setbacks that started to stack up against them in the Coral Sea, Midway, Guadalcanal, Milne Bay and Kokoda. Because of their dominance at this point and the fear of their zealotry, Japanese prisoners were considered a significant security threat. Partly because of this, the Cowra Prisoner of War Camp could in no way be described as a holiday park and it is difficult to express today the level of tension that existed in the camp during these years. As would be seen, this camp held extremely tough and determined individuals. This real threat from the Japanese prisoners was spectacularly confirmed not only by the subsequent breakout in August 1944, but by war's end, where it was discovered that Cowra held no less than 32 suspected Japanese war criminals. These 32, rather than being returned to Japan with the rest of the prisoners in March 1946, were instead taken to the war crimes trials in Rabaul.

* * *

Lees, the guard party and Naka stood outside the southern main gate to Broadway. Once inside there would be a short walk to the next gate, being the entry to the officers' compound. Before the first gate was opened, Lees noticed that Naka was persistently scratching. Lees knew that both Allied and Japanese soldiers in New Guinea had suffered from a range of skin complaints: athletes' foot, a myriad of fungal infections around the crotch area, face and scalp, and impetigo. But a cursory examination by Lees confirmed that Naka had scabies, a contagious skin condition caused by mites. Also called 'jungle rot', 'New Guinea crud' and 'the creeping cruds', the condition required medical treatment so, instead of joining his fellow officers, Naka was immediately taken by Lees to the Regimental Medical Officer building from where he was sent straight to the hospital. Meanwhile the Japanese officers who were expecting Naka's arrival were left standing wondering what had happened as the guard turned around and departed. A minor and routine medical incident had inadvertently provided Naka with an opportunity to commence some of his mischief. This also led to a chain of events that would provide the ways and means for his comrades in arms to resolve their shame.

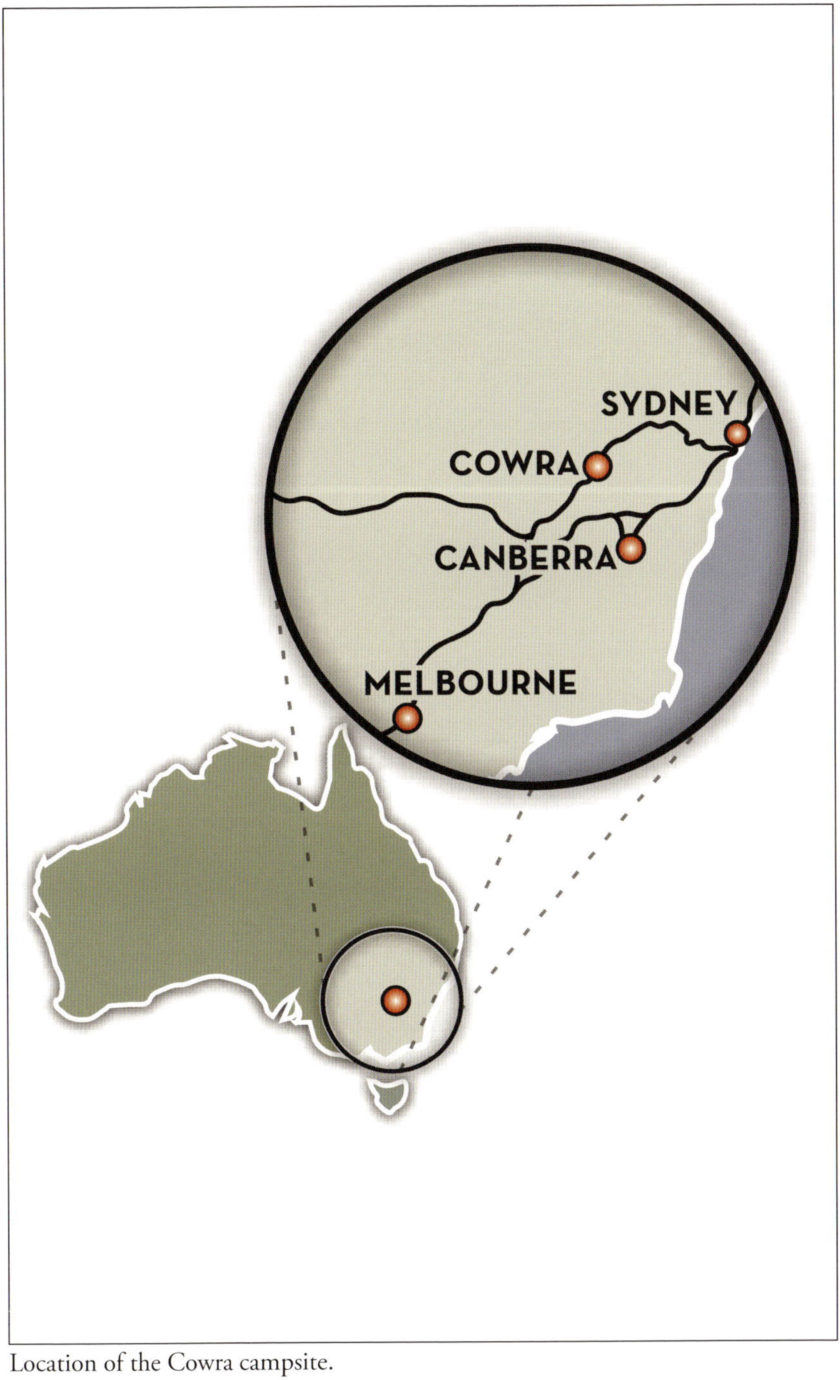

Location of the Cowra campsite.

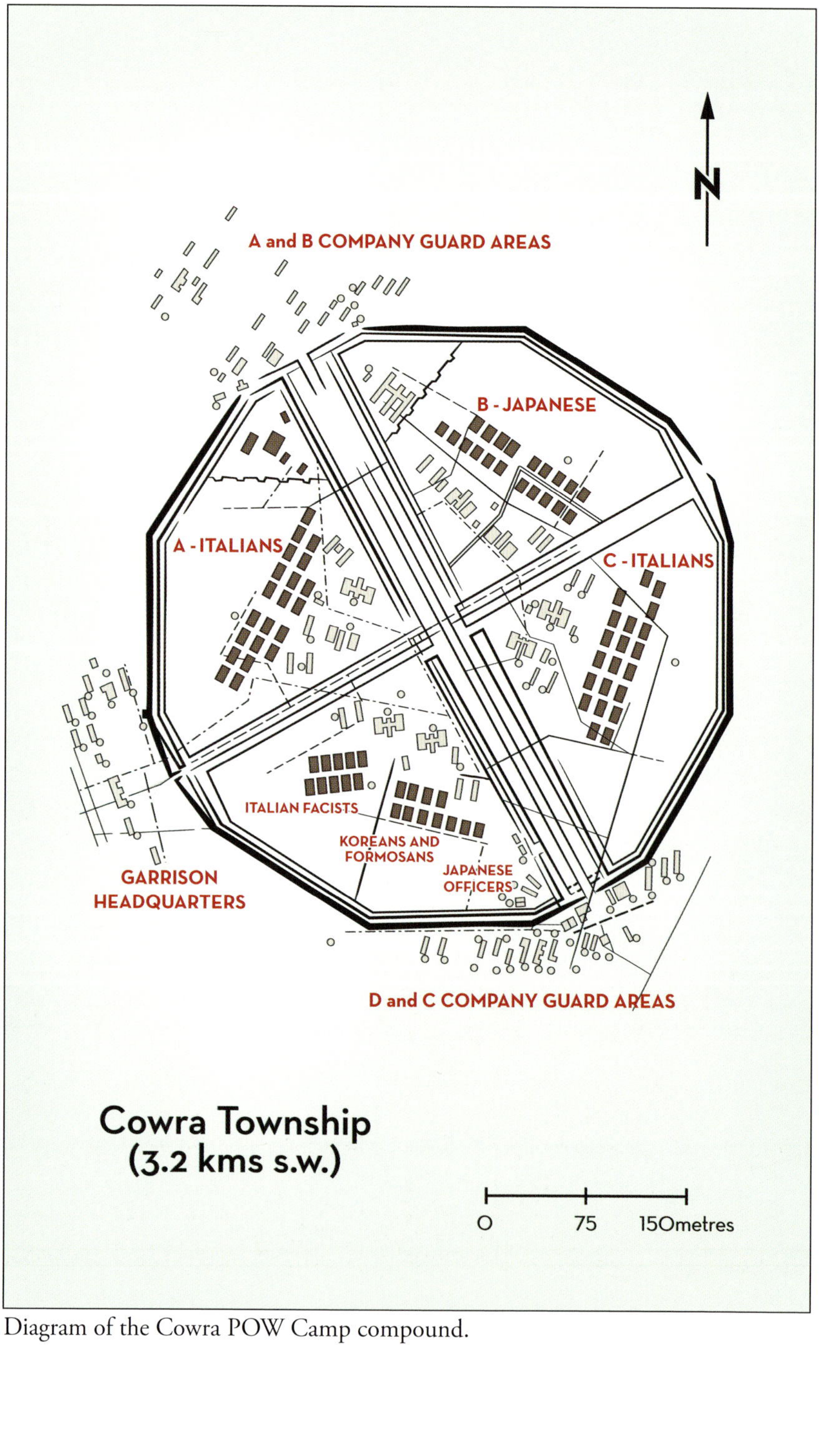

Diagram of the Cowra POW Camp compound.

Official Australian photographers took these photographs of captured Japanese prisoners of war. While obviously posed, they nevertheless show that once the battle was over, there was genuine care provided for these men. AWM 014218.

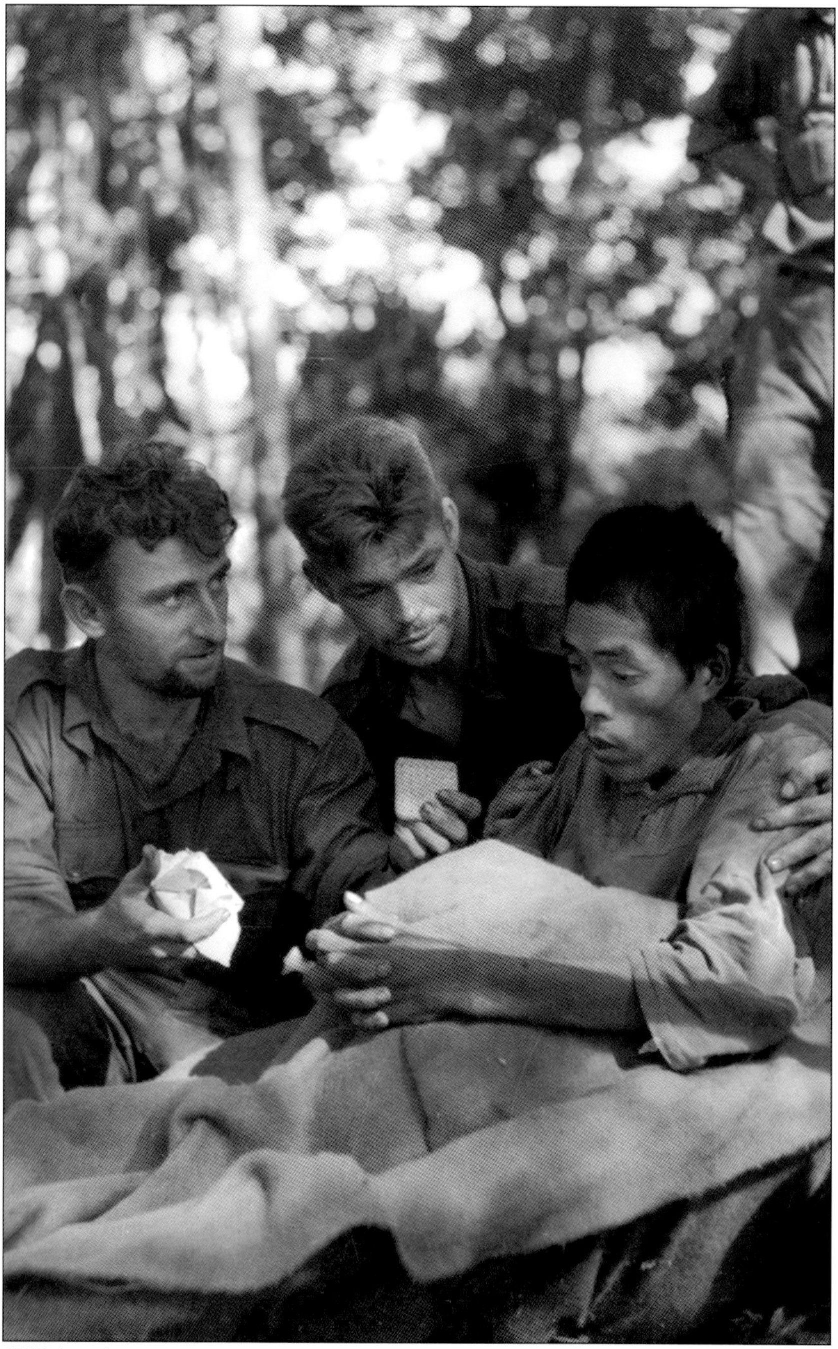

AWM 026825.

AWM 016314.

AWM 058653.

AWM 058789.

AWM 151065.

The view from the guard tower outside the perimeter of A Compound. The guard tower outside B Compound is seen opposite. At its base is a dog kennel with a black and white canine in residence. The double gates of the northern end of Broadway can be clearly seen as can the low security fences. The isolation ward of the single tent where Naka spent time can be seen to the left of the buildings. AWM 064345.

Japanese prisoners of war from Hay and Cowra wait to board the *Daikai Maru* in March 1946. AWM 126121.

Lae, New Guinea. 30 Dec 1944. Senior representative Wysham, Australian Red Cross society issuing comforts to Lieutenant Horoshi, Medical Officer, Japanese Army who is a prisoner of war at the 2/7th Australian General Hospital. AWM 077764.

Balikpapan area, Borneo. 3 Sep 1945. Corporal A.J. Kentwell, interpreter, questioning a Japanese Soldier outside his hut. AWM 115021.

Balikpapan, Borneo. 10 Sep 1945. Rear Admiral T. Nomura, Imperial Japanese Navy, surrendered to Brigadier F.G. Wood, Commander 25th Infantry Brigade, in a surrender ceremony held in the camp area of 2/1st Pioneer Battalion. Shown, Corporal A. J. Kentwell, who acted as interpreter for Brigadier Wood, questioning the Japanese party. AWM 116578.

The late Marekuni Takahara pictured here at the 60 Anniversary of the Cowra breakout. Takahara was one of the batmen involved in the Naka assault incident

Japanese school groups are regular visitors to the POW camp site. On this day in 2014 they were guided by (from left to right) Harvey Nicholson Vice President of the Cowra Breakout Association and President Gordon Rolls, son of guard, Alfred Rolls.

The Italian POW presence is also remembered at the site. Kathy Ryan, Mayor Bill West and Lyndell Rolls lay a wreath at the Italian Memorial in 2016.

Today's replica guard tower at the POW Camp showing the waxing moon as it was on 5 August 1944

Replica Guard tower installed at interpretive area. The tower was built to original specifications. Six towers were originally in place around the camp perimeter.

Aerial view of B Compound. The Japanese attack was directed at the No 2 Vickers Machine Gun.

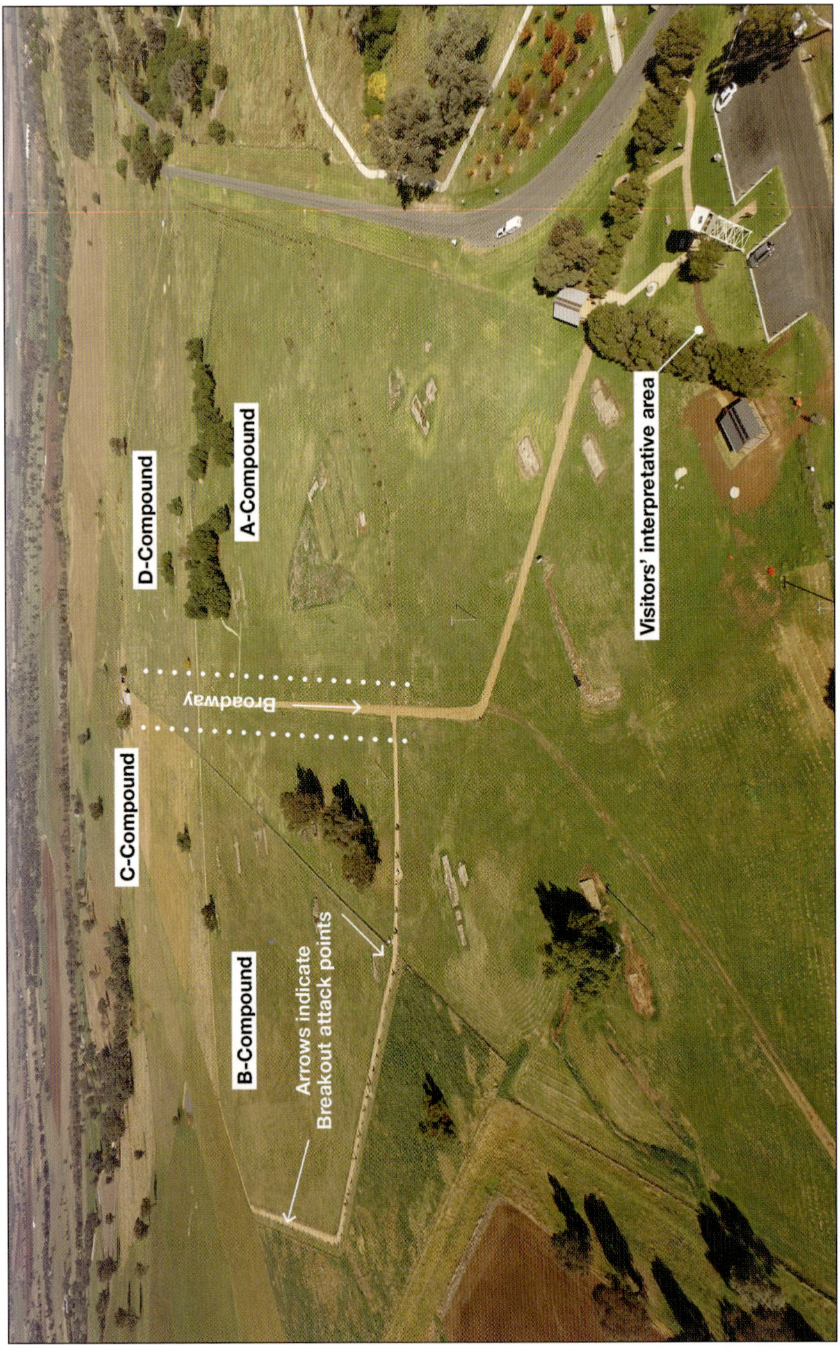

Aerial view of the campsite as it is today. Only the foundations of some buildings remain.

CHAPTER 10
ESCAPE ... TO WHERE?

Naka's entry into the officers' compound was put on hold as it was suspected that his scabies skin condition could infect other prisoners. At the far end of Broadway, hundreds of metres away in D Compound, the Japanese officers were still milling around expecting to see Naka. The scene has been replayed in a dozen prisoner of war movies. The new Japanese arrive, with the current prisoners pressed up against the wire trying to get a look. They grill the new arrivals for information on the outside world and the current state of the war. This gnawing need to know what's happening is one of the great anxieties for war prisoners, and one which Naka could answer. He would have news of the fighting and they would be hoping to hear of expected Japanese victories, but now they would have to wait.

When a prisoner who could not fully understand English was taken to the camp hospital it prompted a call to B Company Headquarters for a translator who would make his way down Broadway to the secured hospital area. This was a functional hospital and the camp had its own doctors and medical staff but only to the extent of treating minor illnesses and injuries. It was built to a wartime budget and anything more complicated than basic care and repair was sent off to the public hospital in Cowra which had its own specially secured prisoner wing.

Naka sat on an army-issue chair facing the doctor, an orderly and the translator. Seemingly calm, his mind and soul were in a turmoil.

'Tell him he's got scabies,' the doctor said, with the translator converting the words into Japanese. Naka knew this already as he understood English and had picked up the earlier conversation. The doctor examined him and found that the small mites had burrowed under his skin and laid eggs. He was now host to a mass of the blind eight-legged creatures that fed on blood and irritated the skin. These mites had taken a heavy physical toll on soldiers on both sides in New Guinea and, for Naka, they were back. The condition that he suffered wasn't the variety of scabies typically caught from sexual contact, often from prostitutes, but what was known as 'clean man scabies'. Those in general good health who bathed regularly were prone to this type and, somehow, Naka's had recurred despite the medical care he had received after capture. This variety appeared as red, itchy patches around the armpits, crotch and back and was contagious but easily treated, though uncomfortable. The doctor ordered the normal treatment for Naka: an application of lindane. This was an agricultural pesticide developed in the 19th century that was used to treat seeds, crops and livestock, and now, apparently, humans.

The brief consultation over, the orderly retrieved the paperwork from the office to admit Naka when he spoke for the first time: 'A gun and a bullet please … May I have a gun and a bullet?' pleaded Naka.

'What?' said the orderly: 'No!'

'You are going to kill me anyway … let me do it … I'll not hurt you … I need to kill myself,' he begged. The doctor noted the outburst, not wholly uncommon in the Japanese when first imprisoned, and entered the details in Naka's file. He instructed the orderly to put Naka in the officers' ward under close watch.

Japanese soldiers had ample opportunities to take their lives in many different ways yet shooting themselves or requesting to be shot was seen as a better choice. While hanging or slicing a vein or artery could have been carried out at any time, Naka in particular seemed to view a military death by shooting as the only honourable end to his situation. He had convinced himself that the Cowra guards were going to kill him and so, before that happened, he had to take the chance to kill himself.

That same evening, before 'lights out', he had penned three notes: last, sad farewells before he ended his life. Just after 10 pm, he slipped quietly out of his bed and pushed the pieces of paper under the covers. He dressed, walked to the toilet, silently approached the window—

calm and preparing to end his life. He climbed up to the window frame and threw himself out. His malaria had returned and confused by his fever and thinking he was in a second-or third-floor building, he would later tell his captors that he was attempting suicide. A shock … the barely 2-metre drop hardly dazed him. Realising that he was still alive he decided to attempt to escape the camp perimeter. During his brief time at Cowra he had observed and taken in what he could see around him, making particular mental notes concerning the security situation, distance from buildings to the wire and the height of the fences. He had also noticed the antics of a four-legged accomplice. Undetected, he made his way to the inside fence under one of the Observation Towers, climbed up the wire, and then clambered up and over the outer fence. Outside the main perimeter, he ran through the guards' tent lines and out past the eastern side of Cowra and began heading towards Sydney along the main highway.

In the meantime, Orderly Sergeant Jim Baillie, on duty that night in the hospital, found an empty bed and sounded the alarm. The duty officer noted in his report: 'Escapee: Name Unknown, speaks little English, height 5 feet 1 inch, slim build, rather good looking for a Jap(!), good features, 25 years of age, dark brown eyes, pair of red Field Dress Trousers, singlet, white hat, tan boots.' As the report notes, the prisoners were all supplied with excess Australian army uniforms that had been dyed in the official colour 'magenta'—red or maroon. The Japanese hated this colour and its associations and did whatever they could to change it, sometimes boiling their uniforms for hours in a mixture of water and ashes.

Meanwhile in his accommodation hut outside the perimeter wire, Intelligence Corps Warrant Officer Lionel Boorman had been hoping for an early night after dealing with a number of unruly and recalcitrant Italian prisoners that week. The Italians were generally more emotional than fanatical—young Latin males feuding with other prisoners and often involving regular fights between royalists and fascist factions. Interviews with these prisoners frequently supplied information about the intrigues and conspiracies within the Italian compounds. They were mostly not dangerous situations as many of the Italian soldiers had been unwilling conscripts into Mussolini's army and were petty but disruptive. In fact Australian officials like Boorman were astounded to later discover that some of the Italians were using their 'prisoner wages' to purchase Australian war bonds!

Boorman had been about to put on his pyjamas when he heard two shots, the pre-arranged 'alarm' signal for all camp personnel to come to 'alert'. He had been rostered for 'callout' that night in case of an emergency and he and another officer ran to their designated posts on the perimeter of B Compound. Naka was already outside the camp and had been seen running quickly over the hills to the main Sydney road. The garrison notified the Military Training Camp that was located on the other side of Cowra and it immediately dispatched soldiers in trucks. They, along with the local Volunteer Defence Corps, had guessed correctly that Naka was heading east. Boorman had received little military training before arriving in Cowra and felt extremely 'unsoldierly'. He was now being ordered into the back of an army truck and heading out to the Sydney road. He mused at the time on the incongruity of it all: 'What was an articled clerk from a small firm of Sydney solicitors doing chasing Japs in the middle of the night?'

Boorman's truck bumped along the road heading east, with four soldiers with pick handles and one with a rifle. Pick handles were a common 'tool' at Cowra but not for digging, and they had developed quite a reputation at the camp. A short time before Naka's arrival, some Japanese prisoners had refused to attend the compulsory morning parades. Discussions with the Japanese hut leaders had failed to resolve the issue. The Military Camp was contacted and subsequently a fleet of ambulances and lorries arrived. The gates at the end of Broadway were opened and the vehicles drove slowly down to B Compound which held the Japanese prisoners. With much deliberation, a number of battle-worn and tough instructors from the Military Camp jumped out of the trucks. They made a dramatic show of inspecting the ambulances and then, rolling up their sleeves, retrieved pick handles from the backs of the lorries. Yelling at the top of their voices they charged into B Compound and launched themselves into the huts.

The Japanese prisoners immediately exploded out the other end of the huts and quickly formed their muster parade. There was no recurrence of this problem ever again at Cowra.

Naka's pursuers now drove along the Cowra–Blayney road eastwards towards the village of Woodstock, branching off now and then to search the back roads and vehicle tracks. When they came to a lonely farmhouse it was suggested by one of the senior non-commissioned officers that, seeing as they had missed dinner, the farmer's wife might make them some sandwiches! 'Boorman, go and ask what's-her-name, if she might help us out.' So he jumped off the truck with his pick handle and walked toward the farmhouse with the driver yelling out: 'We'll go back to the main road and have a look 'round and come back later for dinner,' and he drove off. This anecdote, as related by Boorman later, suggests a somewhat limited concern as to the seriousness of this unique situation—the first-ever escape of a Japanese prisoner during World War II in Australia. While it may be defended as exemplifying the typical Australian 'she'll be right' attitude of the time, these actions also displayed a certain negligence and disregard for a major security breach.

It was, for Boorman, a most comical situation. He was now on his own in the night, outside a farmhouse in the country with a pick handle. Understandably a little apprehensive, he walked up to the homestead, which was in total, still darkness. After waking the farmer and his wife and telling them his story, he asked about the sandwiches. The farmer's wife was pleased to help and got on with making them. Alarmed, she turned to her husband 'Mother is alone—we had better go over there.' Boorman, who didn't want to be left at a darkened farmhouse with only a pick handle, asked, 'Do you mind if I come as far as the main road with you?' The couple dropped him in the middle of the road and drove off along a track through a paddock towards the mother's house. He admitted many years later that he felt 'pretty damn silly' about the whole incident.

Here he was, standing alone on a country road at night with a pick handle in one hand and a packet of sandwiches in the other, trying to recall the few lessons of unarmed combat he had learned during his preliminary training and wondering where Naka might be. After a while, he saw headlights coming towards him and his first thoughts were that his colleagues might mistake him for Naka, but he needn't have worried; Naka was already on the truck. Naka had waved the truck down hoping to get a lift, not realising it was the army truck out searching for him. After picking up Boorman, the guards gave Naka a sandwich and the truck headed to camp. While eating the sandwich, he again asked to be shot.

A telegram from the Cowra camp to the Prisoner of War and Internee section at the NSW Line of Communications Headquarters noted that Naka had been recaptured at 2.50 am on 7 April 1943. He was now in custody and an investigation began. A search of Naka's bed found the three notes. One was a 'soldier's song' composed by Naka; another was a note to his friends Yamashita, Kumaya, Terada, Kondo and Asahara saying: 'I will pray for you, as I have lost a lot of men there is no other way to go, so don't think badly of me.' The third note was: 'Sakamoto, please forgive me, I've lost a lot of my men.'

A long and complex formal process was now undertaken to deal with this 'problem' prisoner. Another telegram was sent off the same day by Group Commandant, Lieutenant Colonel Monty Brown, advising that a court of inquiry was to be convened immediately. This inquiry would not commence until all the parties had been organised; everything was to be 'by the book'. Correspondence and instructions were dispatched from the camp to Sydney and Melbourne and then back again. The court of inquiry's terms of reference were:

- What were the circumstances attending the escape of Lieutenant Naka from the Cowra camp?
- Were the precautions against the escape of the prisoner adequate and proper in the circumstances?
- Were the methods adopted for his recapture in accordance with instructions?
- Is there any reasonable ground for complaint by the prisoner in respect of his treatment before his escape and after his recapture?
- Any other relevant matters.

Due to the unique circumstances at that time, this inquiry carried far more importance than just an investigation into an ultimately failed escape by an obscure Japanese lieutenant. The army and the Australian Government were acutely aware of the fact that more than 20,000 of its own men and women were being held prisoner by the Japanese. In short, Australia feared Japanese retaliation on its own captured troops, nurses and civilians, should it ever be seen to mistreat a Japanese prisoner, either physically or mentally. For this reason, the Protecting Power for the Japanese Government (the Swiss Consulate in Sydney) was to be informed of all 'necessary matters'. As revealed later, this only applied to those matters considered absolutely necessary.[20]

Mentally troubled and affected by malaria and scabies, Naka clearly needed substantial medical treatment and supervision. But he was also an officer and, when recovered and after serving time for the escape, he would be allowed to be accommodated with the other Japanese officers. An officer suffering from malaria, scabies and serious mental health issues who was intent on suicide certainly presented a challenge for the limited facilities available at Cowra camp. The solution to this problem was somewhat unusual but had a certain crude elegance. A photograph of B Compound taken in 1943 shows a small, white tent in the corner of B Compound close to the hospital; it was the 'isolation ward' that was Lieutenant Maseo Naka's new home. It was surrounded by barbed wire to keep him secure but, importantly, it was also visible and close to the hospital. Here, he could be kept under close observation and also receive medical treatment.

Orderly Sergeant Baillie was back on duty at the hospital after Naka's escape and noticed his seemingly improved mood and constant singing even while restricted to his special tent. After a day or so, Jim asked his Korean orderlies what Naka was singing about. Was it a folk song or a lament … what was it? The Koreans replied wryly: 'It is not a folk song or anything like that … he is singing information. He is telling the Japanese in B Compound what he saw in the outside world

20 The Swiss were not oversupplied with information. Following the breakout in August of the next year, Len Whiteley, the Mayor of Cowra was asked to delay the Swiss representative's arrival at the camp. This he did, with he and his wife offering the Swiss representatives many cups of tea and coffee.

when he escaped'! This incident, farcical as it was, was an intelligence coup and may have planted the first seed in the minds of the Japanese that escape was not only possible but perhaps a lot easier than first thought. That seed would grow into the events of August 1944.

In preparation for the court of inquiry, Group Commandant Lieutenant Colonel Monty Brown prepared a report to the Prisoner of War and Internee section of the NSW Line of Communications in Sydney. During the course of the inquiry, the court inspected the camp area three times. On the last occasion, Naka willingly accompanied them in what must have been quite a bizarre situation, offering to show them how he had escaped—an offer they could not refuse! The court hearing commenced with the witnesses providing their testimonies. After all the information had been collated, a clearer picture emerged as to how Naka had escaped. He had occupied Bed No. 2 in Ward 1 of B Compound Hospital. He was witnessed by one of the orderlies close to 'lights out' next to his bed smoking a cigarette. The orderly left the ward to take a late delivery of meat from the local butcher which he took to the kitchen. The prisoner patients were counted every 30 minutes but, when the orderly returned, he found that only 84 out of the 85 were present. An officer was immediately called and, when he arrived at Naka's empty bed, other Japanese patients volunteered: 'Officer go through window'. In simple terms, Naka had gone to the toilet and jumped out of the window, falling into a bush which broke his fall. He then made his way to the wire and through the fence.

When the court of inquiry called Naka, he volunteered to show them how he had achieved his remarkable feat. The court had been advised that Naka had written another note which said 'I am good at escape.' Through a translator, he was duly sworn in and stated that he had been well treated in the camp and was prepared to tell the court how he had escaped. The court adjourned to the compound and Naka proceeded with his demonstration, but not before the guards were at the ready in case the re-enactment turned out to be another escape. He climbed through the inner guard fence, walked across the intervening space, climbed over the entanglements and commenced to walk along the top of the wires supporting the entanglements in the 'manner of a tight rope walker'. Jumping off the wire he picked his way through the entanglements, reached the outer fence and climbed over. The time taken for the exercise was two minutes and forty seconds exactly. More disturbing, there was no damage to his clothing or his person. The court members also noted that the prisoner's movements were quite unhurried and calm. When he was asked whether he had had any tight rope training he said 'no', but for entertainment, he had 'done a lot of training on the Australian wire at Singapore' presumably referring to the barbed wire barriers the 8th Division AIF had placed to defend the city.

More than 60 years later, Jim Baillie, the orderly sergeant in the hospital, recounted that Naka, in the short time that he was in the camp, had studied a small black and tan dog by the name of 'Tiny' and how it often made its way through the wire entanglements. This intrepid pet belonged to guards Mick Nolan and Ned Duffy. Dogs appear to have been tolerated at the camp, but only as pets and dogs were not used in any military sense. This had become a significant issue when Australia complained via the International Red Cross to Germany after Australian POW had been bitten by guard dogs. The Germans uncharacteristically agreed that dogs would not be used to enforce discipline and Australia reciprocated.

Naka told the inquiry that apart from the 'tight rope act', he had escaped by essentially copying what the dog had done. The court members were clearly horrified at the low standard of security arrangements at the camp. Specifically, the lighting appeared to be completely ineffective as the guards had not seen Naka approaching the wire under their noses. One of the guards at the inquiry muttered to his mate, wondering if the dog would be charged as well. Nothing more is known of Tiny and whether he was used to test other areas of the perimeter.

The court considered all of the evidence and found that Naka had escaped from an unguarded window; climbed through a 6 feet (1.83 m) high fence of single barbed wire; over two more fences and barbed wire entanglements; and was then able to make his way to the main road to Sydney. The court found that floodlighting in the camp was ineffective, thereby leaving the bulk of the compound area in darkness. The security fence wires had also sunk because the supporting posts had leaned inwards and, in some cases, had dropped the wire to a height of only 2 feet 6 inches (750 mm). The Dannert wire (rolled entanglements of barbed wire) were ineffective as weeds had grown through them to the extent that, in places, they totally obscured the sentries' view. The guards' tents were also too close to the outside wire, thereby allowing any escaping prisoner to conceal themselves in the lines as Naka had done.

After considering the report from the court of inquiry, Brown and Timms met to discuss the situation. These were two very different men. Brown had joined up as a light horseman in WWI and was then seconded to the Indian Cavalry, where he stayed and served on the North West frontier, returning to Australia in 1922. He was known as a true gentleman with a trim and orderly military mind. Timms was a successful author and known for his love of conversation, whisky and a general affection towards his Italian prisoners. Both treated the security issue extremely seriously and, following the inspection of the camp perimeter, they agreed that the situation was unsatisfactory. A terse letter was then penned and sent off to their superiors at Victoria Barracks expressing their deep concerns for the security of the camp and suggesting appropriate remedies. Brown, a respected career soldier, knew the arcane methods of army decision-making and stressed in all his representations that an excuse of lack of funds not allowing such works was 'intolerable'. Brown was also strident in demanding that the Cowra situation be rectified and, if not, future breaches would not be his responsibility. The cat was now amongst the pigeons and the Deputy Adjutant General instructed those down the line to take action immediately on Cowra's security. In his letter to NSW Headquarters he noted: 'The prisoner spent possibly two minutes negotiating the security fences and during that time, his presence was undetected.' The Senior Engineering Officer (Security) was ordered to Cowra to report on the ways and means of fixing the problem. In the end the fences were repaired but their height was not increased until after the breakout in August 1944.

CHAPTER 10

The court of inquiry completed its work and Naka was sentenced to 28 days confinement in the garrison area detention cells. The intelligence report for that week noted Naka saying that 'he was feeling very lonely and depressed and wanted something to read.' Naka was told in no uncertain terms by his guards that he was being punished for his escape and being lonely and depressed was exactly what they intended should happen to him! The report noted that he had not been given any reading material. When he was released on 4 May 1943 he was transferred to the Japanese Officers' Compound D. No doubt everyone at the camp hoped that this would be the end of Lieutenant Naka's extracurricular activities. Such thoughts were in vain; he was only warming up!

He was returned to hospital on 23 May with a recurrence of his malaria and, on one occasion, was found to have been out of his ward without permission. He was told to return to his bed. He initially refused, but then returned reluctantly after being told that a guard would be called. Naka had stated that he would 'go over the wire again.' After he had recovered, he was discharged on 6 June 1943 and was returned to D Compound under escort. He absented himself from the parade that evening, claiming that he had a headache. The intelligence section at Cowra was particularly interested in Naka's time at the hospital. Part of their role was to shut down any communication channels between the officers and other ranks (ORs). By faking a medical condition, an officer could engineer a stay in the hospital and relay messages to the other patients, hence the rule that officers and other ranks be restricted to separate wards. Likewise, contact could be made with those in detention by manufacturing an incident where a prisoner was sent to the cells. He could then pass on information to those who needed it. A minor infringement would result in seven days of detention but, depending on the importance of the information, it could be considered a worthwhile investment.

It was in this same week that the intelligence section discovered that the Japanese prisoners of war throughout the camp intended celebrating the recent sinking of the Australian ship *Centaur*. This information was seen as being extremely provocative as the *Centaur* was an Australian hospital ship clearly marked with large red crosses and other insignia indicating it as being a non-combatant. It was sunk in the early morning of 14 May 1943 by the Japanese submarine I-177, commanded by Lieutenant Commander Hajime Nakagawa, with the death of 268 of its 332 crew and passengers. He had sunk three ships early in the war but, unfortunately for him, one of them was another Japanese submarine, with the loss of 81 sailors. He was dealt with as a war criminal after the war and spent years in gaol.

The Japanese provoked the Australians in other ways, such as demanding that they take off their shoes before entering their huts. Removing shoes before entering certain buildings, particularly homes and temples, is a common practice in Japan but the demand that it be done in the Cowra camp was seen for what it was: an attempt to control the Australians. Their demand was soon rejected with a flat refusal, with the authorities stating in plain and simple terms that the camp was run under Australian conditions and not those dictated by prisoners of war!

Some information revealed to the Australians by Japanese prisoners of war astounded them. Corporal Duncan Chapman, who was in charge of the Cowra camp rations, had been given a sheepskin vest by one of the Italians. A Japanese prisoner of war asked Chapman if he could get him one. 'Where would I get one?' Chapman replied. The Japanese then told him he could pick one up from Roger's Meatworks at Orange! How did he know that? Chapman found out that this man knew New South Wales well, as he had worked in York Street, Sydney, before the war.

Each morning since he had been made Acting Camp Commandant, 53-year-old Captain Lees inspected the Japanese officers in D Compound. This compound was used for different purposes throughout the camp's operational life and was separated into the sub-units titled D1, D2 and D3. From 1941–47, it would hold Japanese officers, fascist Italians, and Indonesian political prisoners. Koreans and Formosans (Taiwanese) attached to the Japanese Army were separated from the Japanese in B Compound as they had previously been attacked and abused by the Japanese. While no communications were allowed between the diagonally opposite D and B compound areas, those Japanese who were familiar with semaphore were able to pass on messages very effectively.

Naka, meanwhile, had not become a model prisoner by any standard. Because he had escaped, a special dossier was being prepared with a report on 18 June 1943 noting that he was continuing to adopt an 'obstructive attitude'. On three successive days he had absented himself five times from roll calls using the following excuses: 'in the lavatory', 'taking a shower' and three times 'in bed'. The D Compound sergeant tracked him down demanding an explanation. Naka was defiant, stating quite openly that he intended to escape again and he let everyone around him know that after the war the sergeant's throat would be cut.

While tempers and temperament waxed and waned behind the wire, some incidents were hotter than others. Around the same time another officer, newly arrived Lieutenant Oikawa, appears to have stirred up an idea in the heads of his fellows—that of celebrating Japan's Navy Day. Through semaphore they let the others in B Compound know of the plan and ordered them to refuse to work. Officers did not have to work; however, other ranks were required, within reason, to undertake duties as directed. Semaphore messages continued and B Compound leader, Tadeo Minami, who bore the disgrace of being the first POW ever captured by the Australians (his plane crash-landed on the first raid on Darwin), fronted the B Compound sergeant. 'If you come this afternoon to arrest the men who would not work, you will need to bring a machine gun.' The Australians had been challenged and were not averse to using some muscle now and then to sort out intransigent prisoners but on this occasion they let the incident pass.

Naka and others continued their misconduct, which eventually escalated into the event that would change his and their lives forever. Camp Cowra's problems were only just beginning.

CHAPTER 11

A MATTER OF HONOUR

In the humdrum routine that characterised life at Cowra POW Camp, Saturday, 24 July 1943 was just another day for 53-year-old New Zealander Captain Leslie Lees, as he inspected the Japanese officers' compound. Lees had been a motor mechanic before joining up in 1914, serving in Gallipoli, Egypt and France before finishing his service as a corporal in the NZ Provost Corps (Military Police). With a distinguished military record, he had been awarded the Meritorious Service Medal and the French Award, Medaille d'Honneur avec Glaives (bronze). After the war, he moved to Australia and became a police officer with the *Criminal Investigation Branch* in Sydney before again enlisting in 1940 in the Provost Corps and moving to Cowra. Appointed an officer at the POW camp, he and his wife set up house at 72 Liverpool Street. Lees had a solid background as a soldier and police officer and appears to have been well thought of at the camp. The Japanese officers, following a previous inspection by the International Red Cross, asked its representative Dr George Morel to express their gratitude to him.

While the regular parades and inspections generally went off without incident, Lees was still accompanied on his rounds by five other soldiers. On this day, they were Sergeant Fraser, Corporal Arkey, Privates Hunn and Kelly, and Lieutenant Louwisch, a Japanese-speaking "White Russian" who acted as interpreter. The Japanese officers, as required, stood on parade in a single line and Lees made the inspection, asking if there were any complaints. Maseo Naka who had returned from his time in detention was the first to speak, in English, demanding to know what sentences were imposed on the Japanese batmen (officers' personal servants). They had been dealt with by

Captain Lees some days earlier as they failed to appear for the 4.30 pm roll call. Lees stiffened at this outburst and, knowing Naka's chequered past at the camp, advised him bluntly that one had received a sentence of 28 days' detention and the others were to serve 21 days each. The 28-day sentence was for Marekuni Takahara, a shared batman for the officers in D Compound, meaning that he was also Naka's batman. Takahara in reality had been a navigator gunner in a flying boat which had been shot down over northern Australia.

After capture, he transformed himself into "Ichiro Takata", humble steward from a sunken Japanese merchant ship. He successfully maintained this subterfuge throughout the war. Because he had professed to be a steward, it was thought that he would make a good batman and was therefore allocated to the officers' compound. He, along with the other batmen, had only recently been in detention a few days prior to Naka's protest.

When interviewed many years later, Takahara remembered Naka as a soldier deeply steeped in militaristic nationalism and acutely distressed that he had been unable to die for his country. Takahara believed that this was the cause of his general petulance and seeming inability to agree with anyone, including the other prisoners. Takahara was, throughout this time, almost certainly acting as a go-between from the other ranks as he moved daily between his quarters in B Compound to the officers in D Compound. This role was of central importance in passing information between the two groups and maintaining the loyalty of the men to their officers.[21]

For now though, Naka was angry and yelled at Lees in English: "Sentences too long!" Lees countered directly: "It is none of your business." Naka asked if he could go to prison in the batmen's place. Lees told him that he could not, but Naka continued to argue the point. Lees, intent on putting a halt to the matter, told him flatly: "No, I will not discuss it any further" and the parade was dismissed. Turning to leave the compound with the rest of the party, Naka yelled: "I want to go to prison."

---

21 Takahara later became a great friend of the people of Cowra and visited the town many times to promote reconciliation.

Lees's party stopped at the gate waiting for it to be opened when Naka ran to Lees's left and, without warning, punched him squarely on the jaw, knocking him sideways and dislodging his glasses and cap. Lees, recoiling and turning around, saw Naka running back to the group of Japanese officers yelling out the word "ashamed", apparently to indicate the motive for the unprovoked attack. Private Hunn immediately arrested Naka, taking him into custody, with Lees ordering the guard party to leave the compound. Captain Lees went immediately to the camp hospital where the examining medical officer found that he had suffered substantial swelling on his left jaw but no fracture.

Other insights into the situation at Cowra POW Camp in 1943 can be gleaned from the writings of someone who was there at the time. Kenneth Seaforth Mackenzie was a guard at Cowra and, after the war, published his novel *Dead Men Rising*. Although a work of fiction, his story contains a number of insights into Naka's situation and other observations on the camp at Cowra that were incisive and detailed. While his perceptive observations were contained within the creative context of a novel, they were certainly centred on his time as a guard at the camp over two years, less several periods when he was 'Absent Without Leave'. The relationship between Naka and his courier batman Marekuni Takahara features heavily in the novel with the description of a character: 'That little lieutenant who shaves every morning outdoors with a mirror is a signaller, and he shares a batman.' Mackenzie goes on to identify this individual as having 'struck an officer' and that: 'even as a Japanese, he was very good looking.' Naka's handsome features, describing him as 'almost pretty' and 'good looking for a Jap', were often mentioned in his files.

The novel *Dead Men Rising* was written by Mackenzie in 1949 and published in 1951. This was just six years after the war and well before the 20-year embargo on official records was lifted allowing historians, journalists and writers access to these invaluable documents. Despite this, Mackenzie's personal recollections, as revealed in his work, align closely to 'official' versions of the escape published later by Hugh Clarke in *Breakout at Cowra* and in Harry Gordon's work *Die Like the Carp*.

CHAPTER 11

In *Dead Men Rising*, our Lieutenant Maseo Naka becomes 'Lieutenant Yoshiro I' with 'I' being a common enough Japanese name. Employing the actual incident of Naka striking Captain Lees for dramatic purposes, Mackenzie in his novel develops an interplay which parallels the episode involving the real-life characters. In the novel, Captain Lees becomes 'Major Collace' and the enigmatic and real-life Manchurian-born interpreter at the camp, Oleg Negerevich (also known as: Norvall) becomes 'Orloff'. The character 'Collace' is portrayed in the novel as a small, evil-tempered officer, generally disliked by his men because of his bullying of juniors. There is no evidence to believe that Lees possessed any of these traits. Physically, Lees was approximately 5 feet 10 inches (about 178 cm), quite tall for the time, a point noted in Naka's subsequent trial. Also, there is no evidence that he provoked or goaded Naka in any way leading up to the assault. Either Mackenzie didn't like Lees personally, or he developed these negative character traits in 'Collace' simply as a mechanism for heightening the levels of conflict between the characters.

Whether based on the reality of the situation at Cowra or not, the novel reveals that while there is little sympathy from fellow officers for Collace, there is a recognition that a serious security situation has developed at the camp from the unprovoked attack. The character of Orloff reveals this insight, but it is one that the Australian officers take some time to grasp. He believes that Yoshiro's actions in hitting Collace were a dangerous expression of the Japanese frustration at their situation. Orloff says that the prisoners had been waiting for something to happen and that Yoshiro had delivered on this with his attack on an officer. His attack, whether intended or not, was the signal to others for further action.

Had the Australians also not heard the Japanese prisoners baiting them with shouts of 'Singapore' when they approached the compound, reminding them of their greatest defeat at the hands of the Japanese? The crude insolence and awkwardness of the assault by Yoshiro on Collace, Orloff says, was a misguided display of bravery by Yoshiro in front of his men. Yoshiro had fully expected and even wanted to be executed immediately. Because this did not happen he was now,

Orloff says, the unhappiest prisoner in the camp having lost suicide as his only way to redress the loss of his honour. But while Yoshiro was unhappy with his failure he had inspired others who were now deeply in thought about what possibilities lay in store for them.

Mackenzie then moves the novel to a discussion between Orloff and the Australian officers where he tries to make them understand the Japanese mindset. After this conversation, they now realise that the prisoners laugh at them because of their adherence to the Geneva Convention. Orloff tells them that if an attack on an officer happened in a 'Jap' camp, all of the Australian prisoners, not just the attacker, would be executed. 'Honour' they now comprehend 'is a blunt weapon against dishonour cleverly used.' While hard to determine how much of the novel is based on the events around Naka's attack on Lees, it is easy to believe that death by execution to restore his lost honour was his ultimate aim. It is also most probable that if Mackenzie knew of such matters, that the well-known Japanese intelligence network within the camp was equally apprised of all these issues.

Following the attack on Lees, Naka was now the subject of a court martial under Australian military law. Lieutenant Colonel Monty Brown advised the Prisoner of War and Internee section that two charges were submitted against Naka. The matter had been fully investigated by Major Jarman and a local solicitor, Captain Edgar Moseley, with evidence taken from all relevant witnesses. Brown also noted that Naka was in custody with his general character described as 'indifferent'.

Naka was charged and ordered to appear before a court martial to be convened by Major General Albert Fewtrell set down for 7 September 1943 at Cowra Court House. The charge against Naka, detailed in a letter by Monty Brown on 2 July, was for: 'Using personal violence to an officer employed in connection with a Prisoner of War Camp.' The alternative charge was the well-known but less serious offence of: 'an act prejudicial to good order and discipline among prisoners of war.' A letter to Naka outlined that he would be given a summary of evidence and a copy of the charge sheet in Japanese. He was asked to state in writing whether he wished to have an officer assigned to represent him, or whether he wished to choose a legal adviser from the town. While all these slow legal procedures were being implemented, Naka had other ideas.

Another of the camp's Japanese language interpreters, Lieutenant Joseph Louwisch, delivered the translated version of the charge sheet in Japanese to Naka on 25 July. Naka confirmed that he had received the official letter, and requested an interpreter and a counsel for his defence. He said that he did not know any Australian lawyers and understood that his defence would now be appointed by the court. Meanwhile, Naka was being held in detention in Cell No. 11 at the POW camp. Lance Corporal Ayre, a guard on duty there, discovered at 11.55 am on 24 July that Naka had barricaded himself in his cell. He reported this immediately to the regimental sergeant major who, knowing the likely reason for this action, raced to the cell where he found the prisoner's bed jammed against the door. Peering through the grill he saw a knotted towel. They forced the door open and found Naka hanging by the neck by a noose made out of a towel and a leather belt. He was frothing at the mouth and his face was swollen. The sergeant major lifted him up to take the strain and Ayre undid the towel and Naka was carried out and placed on the ground. The medical officer was called and arrived at 12.08 pm and Naka was examined and declared to 'be quite alright'. But for Naka, the proud, damaged soldier who was still desperately seeking redemption through death, everything was far from 'alright'.

CHAPTER 12
COURT MARTIAL

The date had now been set for Naka's trial. General Albert Fewtrell, Commanding Officer for the NSW Lines of Communication Area, sent the obligatory letter to Swiss Consul General Hans Georg Hedinger on 4 August, advising him of the impending hearing. Hedinger was informed that Naka would be represented by a fully qualified barrister but if the consul general preferred another counsel, every attempt would be made to secure their services. These solicitous inquiries displayed far greater concern for the administration of justice than would have been afforded to an Australian-born accused. They were in part simply recognition of the potential for any adverse actions on the 22,000 Australians now under Japanese imprisonment. There was no such request for alternative counsel from Hedinger but Naka, seemingly with a growing awareness and knowledge of the legal procedures impacting on his life, would have a change of heart a little later. Hedinger wrote back to Fewtrell agreeing with his recommendation that Arthur Moverley, a well-known Sydney barrister, would conduct Naka's defence.

Contemporaries remember Moverley as very much a figure of his times. Justice John Slattery, AO, QC, KCSG, when interviewed in 2011 at the grand age of 93, was a distinguished judge having had carriage of a number of significant legal cases over a long career. He remembered Moverley as tall and well dressed with the quiet and deliberate legal manner typical of those involved in equity matters. In the gentlemanly civil law circuits in which Moverley operated, what was most important was convincing distinguished judges on the fine legal points of your case. Common law and criminal barristers, on the other hand, tended to be much more assertive and theatrical in their attempts to sway juries comprised of local community members.

CHAPTER 12

Moverley had graduated from the University of Sydney in 1923 and was an associate to a judge of the Supreme Court, Justice Long Innes. This position said something about Moverley's status and regard in the profession. Being an associate (a legal clerk) assisting a Supreme Court judge suggests that Moverley had good social connections and had also achieved well academically. He was admitted to the bar (the professional body for barristers) in 1928 and developed a reputation in legal circles as a specialist in bankruptcy with a solid and successful practice. One of his notable clients in a case for which he achieved considerable press coverage was the infamous Aimee Belle Edols, a well-known bankrupt who was ultimately sentenced to four years in gaol for contempt of court and fraud. The case in 1934 involved the Commonwealth Crown Solicitor and Federal Attorney, no less, appointing two King's Counsels to pursue Mrs Edols in court over longstanding fraud allegations. Moverley was Mrs Edols's counsel and, although unsuccessful, was believed to have acquitted himself well against the two esteemed King's Counsels. Moverley was appointed in 1937 to the Southern and South Western New South Wales Circuit list as a barrister, with the Cowra area part of his legal rounds. It was in this position that he was appointed to represent Naka in 1943.

In the conservative Australia of the 1930s, Moverley's personal life was not without incident and a touch of scandal. Perceiving in 1938 that his marriage to his wife Evelyn was in trouble, he left her. The unhappy and now abandoned wife brought her legal situation to the Divorce Court of the day, pleading for an order to force Arthur back to the family home. Until the family law reforms of the 1970s, all Divorce Court matters were open to reporting and were staple fare for the gossip pages. Newspapers at the time dutifully reported Mrs Moverley's legal request under 'I want my husband to return to me!' headlines. The remedy of a 'decree for the restitution of conjugal rights' was ordered by Acting Justice Edwards who directed Moverley to either take back or return to his wife. This attempt at reconciliation was shortlived and a divorce via decree nisi (a court order to end a marriage) was declared on October of the same year.

Moverley's career continued and during the war he agreed to defend an Italian prisoner at Cowra POW Camp, Sante Pratico, who had assaulted an Australian soldier. Through his experience in that assault case, he had come to the notice of Judge Advocate Ernest Street, a member of the prominent legal family who handled all military prosecutions. For whatever reason, Moverley's name was put forward to defend another prisoner, a Japanese prisoner at Cowra. Shichijo Shojiro was a contemporary of Lieutenant Naka's from a different unit and had also been captured in New Guinea, on 28 January 1943, just two days after Naka. Both of them were now in the camp at Cowra but Naka was in the officers' compound. Shojiro's offence was to try and grab a loaded rifle from one of the guards while he was on a work detail. He had only been stopped in this attempt through the intervention of two Japanese. After being detained, he had given an apology but this was noted as being insincere. He was off to the detention cells and denied his cigarette ration. With more than 50 per cent of the adult population smokers at this time and the figure far higher for soldiers, cigarettes for a prisoner were a necessity rather than a luxury. Their denial for disciplinary reasons was a severe punishment, pure and simple. Each Japanese prisoner (including the Koreans and Formosans) was issued with free cigarettes. The normal ration for prisoners was 35 cigarettes per man per week with the Japanese prisoners especially addicted to the habit. So powerful was its hold over them that the judicious handling of cigarette rations as reward and punishment was effective in their control and management. A little later, a reduction of the ration came at an interesting time.

Shojiro's action in trying to grab a rifle from a guard, presumably to use it against the Australians, finally and decisively convinced the camp authorities that the Japanese prisoners were simply too high a security risk to be used on work parties. His case did not proceed as he was declared insane and sent to the Gladesville mental asylum.

Naka's case was still progressing. An American naval lieutenant from the Allied Translator and Interpreter Section (ATIS) travelled to Cowra on 11 August to interview Naka and other Japanese prisoners. This interrogation was not connected to the trial; however, Naka was seemingly so impressed with this lawyer from the United States, that two days later he requested that he represent him at trial. This threw the court proceedings into chaos with the NSW Prisoner of War and Internee Section Headquarters considering the request as 'most undesirable'. As well as questions as to his availability, the issue of the legal competency of an American trained lawyer appearing at trial under Australian law arose. How could Lieutenant Barker be expected to be familiar with the legal points of Australian military law that might arise?

While this debate was going on, Naka, who seemed to enjoy frustrating the authorities, now insisted that he be separately court martialled for his most recent attempted suicide. A frustrated Colonel Brown wrote to the NSW Prisoner of War and Internee Headquarters and received a reply from Lieutenant Colonel Street advising that in fact a charge could be made against Naka under Regulation 47 of the National Security (Prisoner of War) Regulations namely: 'An act prejudicial to the well-being of a prisoner of war, namely himself.' At the time, suicide, whether attempted or even successful, was a crime. Street noted though that it was not necessary that a charge be made against him, unless it was considered by reason of 'matters of policy' that it was desirable to do so. A relieved Monty Brown wrote back suggesting that as Street's advice was that, as it was not necessary to charge Naka, this advice should 'be adhered to'. Brown was becoming increasingly exasperated and frustrated: 'If Naka demands a Court Martial, this will mean that the whole set up for his pending Court Martial (the assault on Captain Lees) will be disorganised entirely,' he wrote. Brown then pushed the point that there was no real purpose in pursuing an additional court martial, noting that Naka couldn't be given a greater punishment than what he was already serving. There would be no separate charge for his attempted suicide.

* * *

Meanwhile, Moverley was still the appointed defence counsel and was scheduled to travel to Cowra. The question as to why Moverley was selected to defend Naka is also relevant. Was Moverley just an average legal performer engaged to do a modest job in defending Naka? This seems unlikely, considering his highly regarded career and that he was heading towards silk (appointment as a King's Counsel). It is possible that he picked up this brief through his connections, or by having performed well in court and being recognised by Judge Street. It seemed of little importance, as there was no doubt that Naka was going to be found guilty of the charge, though he was entitled to a proper defence. There was another interested party in the case: the Swiss. Because of the 22,000 Australians now behind Japanese barbed wire, not only should there be a trial, but it had to be seen to be held with a proper defence. The intricate details of the case would in due course be reported back to Japan.

Hedinger was told that Naka had requested Lieutenant Barker from the US Navy to represent him in his court martial. Hedinger was told though that the prosecutor could object to any person not deemed to be 'properly qualified' to act as defence counsel. An opinion was not offered as to whether an objection was likely and if it would be upheld. The Australians preferred that the Swiss not insist on Lieutenant Barker. Hedinger was also advised that Barker would be in a forward (combat) area at the time of the trial. The Australians added that Barker could not be made available to defend Naka unless the US Navy made special arrangements to have him returned to Cowra. In spite of these impediments, the option to engage Barker was still left open to Naka and Hedinger, who replied to Army Headquarters that: 'should it not be found possible to comply with the wishes of the prisoner in this regard, it would appear that the arrangements mentioned above will have to stand.'

This was the end of Naka's latest manoeuvre and Moverley was confirmed as defence counsel with local solicitor Edgar Moseley prosecuting. Moseley had become a solicitor in Cowra in 1926 and worked in the local law firm of Garden and Montgomerie. He had served at Gallipoli in World War I and was twice seriously wounded in France. His role as an army legal officer with the rank of captain required that he be available 'on request'. The engagement for the defence of an experienced barrister, albeit with expertise in areas other than military court martials, against a less experienced (but well regarded) country solicitor for the prosecution raises questions about whether the authorities were after a desired outcome. Because of the perceived highly sensitive nature of the case, justice must not only be done, but it must be seen to be done. There was no argument about guilt, but rather the final sentence, especially as every word of the case would ultimately be transmitted to Japan.

Naka's cell was small even by prisoner of war camp standards, just 10 feet by 6 feet (3 metres by 1.8 metres) and he was heard to pace nervously up and down its confines until breakfast was served. At 9.15 am on the day of the trial, two guards arrived at the detention block and handed their paperwork to the duty officer to take Naka to the court house in Cowra. His cell door was then opened and he was ordered to stand up. Knowing the procedure, he offered his slightly clenched hands in front and was handcuffed. Experience showed that clenching the muscles would assist in a slightly looser and more comfortable fit of the cuffs when the wrist was subsequently relaxed. The guard party of an officer, sergeant and two soldiers walked him down the building's side ramp to a truck. Naka climbed up, followed by the guards, and in turn the sergeant; the officer went to the car and both vehicles drove off, exiting the camp at its northern perimeter.

The court house in Cowra's main street was built in 1880 and had been designed by New South Wales' most prominent colonial architects James Barnet and Walter Liberty Vernon with courses of English bond sandstock bricks. The elegant Australian Victorian design was typical of New South Wales country towns. It displayed the high windows of the period aimed at providing a measure of cooling air during the hot, stifling days of summer that in Cowra could reach 100 degrees Fahrenheit (38 degrees Celsius). The thick walls, verandas and high windows and ceilings were designed to draw hot air to the top of the room and circulate cooler air with the aim of slightly refreshing the judges, lawyers, accused, and spectators in the court, most of whom were required to wear coats, collars and ties. Across the street was the local police station which had been informed of the court martial and next door was the Returned Soldiers', Sailors' and Airmen's League building. As this was a court martial, the court house staff were dismissed for the day with much muttering about a 'spectacle' taking over their small domain.

The two army vehicles headed down the frighteningly steep hill past the municipal council's water treatment plant and hospital towards the town centre. The incline was considered quite a test for the heavy trucks by their drivers, who often shifted the gears down to a snail's pace as they didn't trust the government-issue brakes. For security, all traffic had been cleared from in front of the court house in Kendal Street and the vehicles turned left and parked in front. The guards were the first out, followed by Naka who was taken in through the stately front doors to the rear courtyard holding area where he was directed to a bench seat where he waited with two guards. His handcuffs were removed and all three relaxed a little and enjoyed the obligatory smoke. A short time later the officer appeared and Naka was taken to the holding cell.

Has such a collection of legal luminaries ever attended a minor assault charge against a war prisoner in a country town before or since? The NSW Judge Advocate, Ernest Whistler Street; Naka's defence counsel, equity court barrister and soon to be a King's Counsel, Arthur Moverley; and President of the Court, Colonel Penfold, who had travelled by rail to Cowra on the day before the trial. When the group arrived, Moverley, along with interpreter Louwisch, went straight to Naka's cell to brief him on the procedures and to make sure that, within reason, he understood what would be happening. The trial was set for one day only. The authorities must have been confident of a result as everyone from Sydney was booked to travel back to Sydney by rail on that same evening, 7 September.

One hour before the trial was to start, Colonel Penfold, together with members Majors Ramsay and Norris and Captains Robinson and Bullock, met in the court house judges' meeting rooms to outline the procedural aspects that were about to commence in the case. Present were Lieutenant Colonel Street as Judge Advocate, Captain Moseley, the local solicitor as the prosecutor, and Moverley as defence counsel. It was 10 am and the members of the court, the prosecution and the defence then filed into the courtroom. Naka's handcuffs had been put back on and he was placed in the dock by the guards who now stood either side with all three now facing the bench. The charges against Naka were read out: 'Using personal violence to an officer employed in connection with a Prisoner of War Camp' and the alternative charge of 'an Act prejudicial to good order and discipline among prisoners of war.' In a case involving alternative charges, the accused can be found guilty of only one but not both; Naka pleaded 'not guilty' to both in Japanese and Lieutenant Louwisch translated.

As in most criminal cases, it is the role of the prosecutor to first address the court laying out the prima facie evidence for conviction. Captain Moseley did this, addressing the court and describing the case as straightforward. 'It will be proved,' he said, 'that Captain Lees was the Camp Commandant; Lieutenant Naka was under his command as a prisoner of war; Captain Lees was carrying out his official duties and that, before leaving the compound, Lieutenant Naka assaulted him.' Moseley added that it would also be proved that the assault was unprovoked and premeditated. In compliance with the National Security Regulations, Moseley tendered the letter from the Protecting Power for Japan, the Swiss Consul General, acknowledging certification that Naka was to be tried by a military court. The first witness for the prosecution was Captain Leslie Lees, telling the court that at 11.30 am he entered D Compound with other soldiers as was customary and the Japanese officers fell in on parade. He then detailed the circumstances of the assault.

Naka's defence counsel, Arthur Moverley, sprang into action in his cross-examination with his years as a barrister in evidence with his confident delivery. In the time-honoured 'best traditions of the bar' he now tried to present a seemingly straightforward incident in the best possible light for the benefit of his client. Moverley did this by seeking to complicate the events surrounding the assault, asking Lees about Naka's first question to him concerning the imprisonment of the batmen: 'Was the fate of the batmen an important issue for Naka?' Moverley wanted to know how Naka asked the question; what words were used, and what was the tone of voice. He asked Lees to repeat the exact words to demonstrate Naka's intonation. Lees attempted this and apologised that he was not very good at imitating voices.

Moverley raised the possibility that confidential information may have been leaked to Naka about the likely fate of the batmen to provoke him. He asked Lees if Naka could have been told by one of the Australians that the batmen would be returned to the officers' compound without punishment. He pursued this point and whether Lees knew of such advice. Why had this act of leniency not occurred? Lees denied that he had any conversation with Naka about this issue prior to the assault. But, on being pressed about the possibility of Naka having said to Lees that he had been told by someone that the batmen would not be punished, Lees admitted that Naka may have said that. Moverley asked about Naka's general demeanour. Lees said that Naka had acted as though he had a peremptory right to discuss the issue of the batmen at length with him. Moverley asked about the way in which Lees dealt with the Japanese officers—did he provoke and antagonise? 'You do not unnecessarily run up against them?'

Lees did not answer the question directly but said that, 'Since Naka had been removed, it has been quite peaceful'.

Moverley then sought clarification about Naka's desire to go to prison in place of the batmen. Lees said he considered that Naka felt he was partly or fully to blame for the batmen's sentence, and so wanted to take their place. Did this mean that Lees believed that Naka's behaviour was motivated by personal concern about the batmen and his own part in their imprisonment? Lees agreed with this notion, but said he was not familiar with the concept of a Japanese officer taking personal responsibility for offences of their servants.

Moverley completed his cross-examination by asking Lees about the effect that Naka's assault had on the other Japanese officers and prisoners. Had they become more confrontational? Lees replied that the demeanour of the other Japanese officers had not changed at the time or since.

It was still the prosecution case and Moseley now questioned the remaining three witnesses: Corporal Arkey and Privates Hunn and Kelly. When Arkey was questioned about whether Naka was courteous when asking Lees about the batmen, Arkey replied that Lees demanded such courtesy and had received it from Naka. On the re-examination of Corporal Arkey, the president of the court asked Arkey if he was a boxing man and whether he would comment on the type of punch delivered to Lees by Naka. Arkey offered that, as Naka was small in stature and Lees was big, the punch did not cause too much discomfort to Lees. Kelly's evidence was similar and he agreed on the character and impact of the punch. The consensus of all witnesses was that the punch came 'around' and not from the shoulder and, because it was aimed at a much larger man, would not likely have 'stung' too much.

It was now the defence's turn with Naka the accused. Naka stated that he held no animosity towards Captain Lees but he felt it was his 'religious duty' to be similarly punished as his servants. Moverley tried to establish Naka's background by asking about his life before the war. Naka pointed out that like most Japanese prisoners, he did not speak about his home nor did he seek to contact any family in Japan. He said that, as prisoners of war, they were already dead, not only in their own eyes, but in the eyes and hearts of Japan. Naka said that they especially felt they had personally betrayed their emperor. He said that they fully expected to be executed on their return to Japan and that their families would be publicly humiliated and ostracised because of their son's shame as a prisoner. Finding Moverley's questions uncomfortable, Naka answered curtly saying that they had no bearing on the matter at hand. The prosecutor asked under cross-examination whether Naka would ever assault a responsible officer in the Japanese Army. Moverley objected to the question, which was disallowed. When Naka was asked what his motive was for striking Captain Lees he stated simply: 'There was no motive … I was angry.'

Prosecution and defence had now concluded their cases and it was time to sum up. Moseley stood and faced the judge's bench saying that his final address would be based only on the facts. He outlined that this was not an ordinary assault and not what is described in a police court as 'assault'. The accused is an officer in the Japanese Army and Captain Lees who was assaulted was the camp commandant and responsible for the good conduct of the men in that compound. The assault took place in the presence of other Japanese officers and there was evidence it could have been seen by prisoners of war in the adjoining compound. The assault was unprovoked. Captain Lees said he did not see the man who struck him but when he looked around he saw the accused so it was definitely premeditated and Captain Lees was taken by surprise, which indicates aggravation. It was an aggravated assault, it was premeditated and it was unprovoked. Captain Lees was acting in his official duties as camp commandant, not as a private individual or soldier and there was no excuse for the assault.

Moseley concluded that these were the only facts arising from the evidence that he wished to place before the court, apart from the reality that the attack was unprovoked and premeditated. 'Naka is an officer and should know better.'

Defending counsel, Moverley, addressed the court advising that the assault was admitted but that there are degrees of crime and, in particular, degrees of assault. He stated in his clear and concise manner that the actual assault resulted in little more than an inconvenience to Captain Lees in that he lost his hat and some portion of his dignity. He emphasised that the position is not as the prosecution had put it. It was not an aggravated assault at all. The real truth was inescapable as the assault arose from Naka's sense of dishonour which is peculiar to Japanese, and, for that reason, the assault might otherwise have been excusable. Moverley is quoted as saying to the court: 'If a person is grievously insulted that may, of course, provide a defence. But while not an excuse, it should be recognised by the court that, because he is Japanese, because he believes in a code of honour, it is a reason for the assault.' Moverley then asked that the court keep in mind that Naka committed the offence out of a sense of religious belief and duty saying: 'That is not an excuse but, if it is acceptable to the court, I submit they still give it the greatest weight.'

Judge Advocate Street summed up by pointing out that the facts were not disputed but the onus was still on the prosecution to prove its case. He said that, while the final address by the defence emphasised the potential for mitigation, matters relating to mitigation of the sentence are considered after guilt is proven. Street said it cannot be 'mitigating' on the evidence on that decision. Simply, he said, the first question was for the court to decide whether the accused was guilty, and the court could only be satisfied in this respect if the prosecution had proved its case beyond reasonable doubt.

The hearing was complete. Street advised that, while it was not specifically laid down that the judge advocate should now retire to consider his verdict, it was the practice that he does so while the court was deliberating on its decision. There was little doubt as to the final verdict and the accused did not have long to wait to hear it. Naka was found 'guilty' on the charge of 'using personal violence on an Australian officer' and 'not guilty' of 'an act prejudicial to good order and discipline'. Despite his best efforts, Moverley must have known that his client would be found guilty, but it is likely he thought the subsequent sentence of 'two years imprisonment with hard labour' was overly harsh. The case was now ended; Street, Moverley and the court reporter boarded the mail train for Sydney at 7.40 pm that same evening.[22]

Naka had now been in custody for 71 days with a further two years' imprisonment with hard labour to be served at the Hay Prisoner of War Camp. The order for imprisonment was confirmed by Major General Fewtrell on 20 September with the Swiss authorities duly informed of the outcome. Naka was escorted under guard from Cowra on 29 September 1943, to the flat and dusty plains of Hay in western NSW.

The Australian authorities could comfort themselves that justice had been served, and an example set for onlooking Japanese prisoners of war. Naka had been given every chance to defend himself. He now left behind him a legacy at Cowra that, less than a year later, would explode in the most horrific way imaginable.

22 Arthur Moverley subsequently remarried and was appointed King's Counsel in 1950. Moverley's practice was entirely bankruptcy matters and so because of the postwar boom, there was not enough bankruptcy work for a silk. Shortly after being appointed, Moverley's practice collapsed and he died at the young age of 49 on 13 February 1952, ironically leaving a bankrupt estate.

CHAPTER 13
OTHER COWRAS

The breakout at Cowra was not unique among Japanese prisoner of war uprisings during World War II. Raised from childhood in a deeply militaristic culture and with a fanatical hatred of capture, Japanese prisoners were always volatile and prone to protests, clashes and uprisings. While the carnage at Cowra with 231 deaths was the worst, it was by no means the first or the only such event of the war.

There were, in fact, major conflicts with Japanese prisoners in three other Allied camps as well as numerous less serious disturbances. These included:

Featherston, New Zealand, 1943—In September 1942, the former World War I army camp on the North Island of New Zealand was re-opened as a prison camp at the request of the United States. Around 900 Japanese prisoners captured during the defeat at Guadalcanal were then interned at the camp. These comprised two main groups: Korean forced labourers attached to the Japanese military forces and a smaller group of about 250 officers and other ranks of the Japanese Army and Navy. The majority of the navy personnel were from the Japanese cruiser *Furutaka*, which had been sunk by a torpedo during the Battle of Cape Esperance at Guadalcanal. There were another 19 surviving crew of the destroyer *Akatsuki* that was also sunk in the Pacific island battle.

The camp was divided into four compounds, with the Koreans and labourers in one compound, the sailors in the second and the officers and other soldiers in the third and fourth compounds. During a sit in protest of 275 of the prisoners in the second compound on 22 February 1943, a standoff developed between the guards and the prisoners who were refusing to work on the construction of a rugby field. The exact sequence of events is disputed but, at some point, a Japanese lieutenant named Adachi was shot and wounded by the camp adjutant. The remaining prisoners then became highly aroused and vocal. Either from an attack by the prisoners or panic among the guards, the sentries opened fire with rifles, submachine guns and pistols. Within barely a minute, 46 prisoners were dead with another 18 later dying from their wounds. A ricochet from a burst of gunfire also killed New Zealand guard Private Walter Pelvin, and several other soldiers were injured by rocks thrown by the Japanese.

A military court of inquiry placed the majority of the blame for the incident onto the Japanese prisoners but also found that there were 'cultural differences' in the camp that had led to the deadly escalation and which needed to be addressed. Among the issues uncovered by the inquiry was the fact the Japanese prisoners were unaware that, under the 1929 Geneva Convention on Prisoners of War, compulsory work was permissible. As in Cowra, the tragic events at Featherston have subsequently encouraged a spirit of reconciliation with Featherston now home to a Japanese-inspired Peace Garden.

Camp Paita, New Caledonia, 1944—This was a transit camp for Japanese prisoners set up by the Americans to mainly hold captured sailors, airmen and soldiers seized or surrendered at Guadalcanal. There was general tension between two groups of the prisoners: the sailors and airmen who were in relatively good physical condition and spirits in contrast to the soldiers, starved and decimated, who were in a terrible state. These two factions had vastly different combat experiences and there was a strong element of bad blood between them. The sailors and airmen were still full of fanatical fighting spirit, but the battered soldiers, who had suffered terrible privations, had essentially given up and now appreciated the relative luxury of the camp. As with the Australians at Cowra and New Zealanders at Featherston, the American authorities had difficulty administering Camp Paita and, like other locations, this was largely due to the general intransigence of the Japanese prisoners.

The camp commandant at the time wrote of the sense of frustration and powerlessness felt by the guards who would take Japanese prisoners out on work parties where the Japanese would simply sit down on the ground and refuse to move, often baring their chests and asking to be shot. The Allies, in dealing with Japanese prisoners, worked on the universal principle that the camps should keep their charges both secure and as calm as possible. In seeking to 'lower the tone' at Paita, the authorities caved in to what appeared at the time to be a number of seemingly inconsequential demands. This approach allowed a perception to develop among the strident and assertive Japanese prisoners that they could control the situation with the 'tail wagging the dog'; they were storing up trouble for the future. A compromise was reached over many of these demands and all seemed well—for a while, anyway. Paita, like Cowra, was subject to interference from above. These were high-ranking staff who did not have any on-the-ground understanding of the difficulties that camp officers had to deal with on a daily basis. The guards also did little to disguise their hatred of the disruptive and volatile Japanese, and took every opportunity to bait and taunt the prisoners, thereby increasing tensions.

Matters had settled down and all seemed relatively peaceful in January 1944 until a group of militant Japanese petty officers arrived. These agitators quickly exhorted their fellow prisoners to rise up and attack the guards. A carefully hatched plan came undone when the leader was told that the Americans had learnt the details of the plot. Unable to launch their bold scheme to storm the camp, capture weapons, kill the guards and enact their plans to capture a submarine, the militants moved to their back-up plot. Simply put, if they could not die in battle, they would suicide. What followed was a gruesome series of suicides ranging from hanging to communal slashing of throats. The Americans were horrified. In total, 24 prisoners died; the camp at Paita closed and all prisoners were relocated to the American mainland.

Bikaner, India, 1945—This was another Japanese prison of war camp which seemed to be operating well and even peacefully; until a hardline faction took over. This clique commenced their endless plotting with Bikaner becoming a true 'test of wills' between the Japanese prisoners, British officers and Indian troops. The specific trigger for the problems at this camp was a persistent refusal by the prisoners to salute Allied officers as required under the Geneva

Convention. This situation escalated during a visit by Admiral Lord Louis Mountbatten, Supreme Allied Commander South-East Asia, who inspected the Japanese prisoners and asked if there were any complaints. One prisoner asked him who he was, a question which was regarded by the camp authorities as the grossest insolence. After Mountbatten's departure, the British officers decided that now was the time to deal with the matter of camp discipline. The commandant demanded that the prisoners now salute him and, when none did, some were sent to solitary confinement. One prisoner subsequently died under the Indian sun, which only provoked the militants further. All the prisoners in solitary confinement were then released, which was held up by the hardliners as a victory but the camp commandant had other ideas. He gave the prisoners one week's grace to recognise the obligation to salute, with them all immediately going on a hunger strike. Three days later, the guards threw in some bread to the prisoners who threw it back, except one who ate some and was summarily strung up and killed by his fellow prisoners. The British had one more try where each individual Japanese soldier was marched up to the commandant and ordered to salute. Those that refused were directly separated and told that they were being transferred to a camp at Quetta near the border of what is now Pakistan and Afghanistan, which was considered to be a real hellhole. The hardliners though fought back before their departure, setting fire to their huts with three choosing suicide in the flames.

This pattern of defiance, stoic resistance and sudden violence was typical of Japanese prisoners throughout the war and yet at Cowra there was a sense of equilibrium—a reasonably peaceful co-existence between captor and captive. This came about due to the methods employed by the Australians. The situation was about to deteriorate.

CHAPTER 14
THE DESCENT

The town of Hay in the Riverina district of southern New South Wales is no metropolis. It's a long way from anywhere and in 1943—hot, dusty, flat and isolated—it would have seemed even further. If the Japanese prisoners transferred to Cowra thought they were at the ends of the earth, those sent to Hay must have envisaged themselves to be at the furthest point of the universe! The camp itself had been built on the town's showground and racecourse and behind the security fence were accommodation huts, internal roads, a water supply and electric lights. Like Cowra, it was originally designed to accommodate Italian prisoners of war. Japanese internees were also being held there but, unlike Cowra, it also held some ethnic Germans. The camp contained three compounds, each with a capacity for 1,000 men. Living conditions were often difficult for these poor souls with long baking hot summer days often reaching 110 degrees Fahrenheit (40 degrees Celsius) and regular dust storms blowing in from the surrounding district's featureless semi-arid grazing country. Due to Hay's isolation and the chronic war shortages suffered throughout Australia, scarcities of materials and supplies regularly included clothing and even personal items such as toothbrushes and razor blades. Nevertheless the prisoners toiled and laboured dauntlessly, operating a highly productive market garden and farm which provided the camp with fresh foodstuffs, including vegetables, eggs, poultry, milk and animal fodder. The hardworking German and Italian internees also established camp schools, handiwork classes and a camp newspaper. They played soccer, built sports fields and even designed a type of currency to be used in the camp.

Naka though was now on his way to Hay and would experience none of the relative pleasures in the generally harmonious camp environment. He had been transferred out of Cowra as his exploits were rightly viewed as a persistent and continuing disturbance to the peaceful but fragile atmosphere that had been painstakingly established in the camp. He had been handcuffed and marched from his cell in the detention block at Cowra and driven to Hay under armed guard. He had been in Hay for only a week when the judge advocate general forwarded a memo on his sentence to the adjutant general on 5 October 1943. He confirmed that the conduct of the trial was correct in all its procedures, but strongly suggested that the 'hard labour' component of the sentence should be voided. He also expressed the opinion that the sentence of two years was excessive and suggested that the punishment be mitigated to 12 months' detention. Again, the solicitous concern for the administration of justice regarding Japanese prisoners was remarkable, no doubt prompted by the ultimately forlorn hope that the same consideration may have been offered to Australian prisoners of war under Japanese rule. One week later the Deputy Adjutant General, Brigadier Urquhart, commuted Naka's sentence to 'detention for two years'. A few days later a letter from the Swiss Consulate was delivered to Naka in his cell giving him the good news. Whatever elation he felt at this reprieve, he concealed it well as it was noted that the information had little effect on him and his mood and behaviour did not improve.[23] Probably thinking that his situation couldn't get any more dire, he was wrong; Naka's life was to take another turn for the worse.

Naka was back in hospital with a recurrence of his malaria on 22 October. His condition showed improvement under treatment and he was returned to his cell on 14 November. His old demons reappeared and he was clearly in a troubled state of mind when the medical officer, Captain William Hillyer, was called to his cell that same afternoon at 5.20. Hillyer reported that Naka had used his razor blade to cut himself in an apparent suicide attempt which included two incised wounds on the outside of his thigh, a cut to the radial artery on his left wrist and a superficial wound to his throat. He was

23 The advices from the Australian authorities to Japan via the Protecting Power certainly reached Japan and are to be found today in the archives in Tokyo.

immediately taken to the camp hospital where the artery was tied off and the other wounds stitched and dressed. He became excitable in the main ward and was relocated to the sisters' office in Ward No. 3 where he was injected with morphine and another sedative. Naka's condition was reported as being 'satisfactory' at 6.30 that evening. The officer commanding the camp hospital at Hay, Major Robert Alcorn, saw Naka at 9.50 pm and noted that he appeared to be in good condition and showed no signs of shock or bleeding. Two days later at 2 pm on 16 November, he was taken back to the detention barracks for observation and further treatment. That same night he created a further incident by yelling, screaming and banging his head against objects in his cell. Major Bill Cummins from the camp made the blunt observation that Naka: 'Appears to be a mental case.'

It appeared to be little comfort to Naka that his sentence had been commuted. In fact his mental health was deteriorating. Camp Commandant at Hay Lieutenant Colonel Charles Thane wrote to the NSW Line of Communications Area (Prisoner of War and Internee) on 28 November advising of Naka's attempted suicide. He added that the senior medical officer was now watching the prisoner over serious mental health issues. Thane also advised that 'further investigation of attempted suicide was not considered necessary.' This was no doubt alluding to Camp Commandant Monty Brown's similar concern at Cowra, that a charge of attempted suicide (being a criminal offence) against Naka, would prompt another unnecessary and ultimately futile court martial.

But Naka's unpredictability was all too much for the Hay authorities. After consultation between various security and medical staff, it was agreed that Naka could not be effectively managed in his present location at Hay. He had been declared 'insane' by the camp's senior medical officer and also a civilian doctor and it was decided to transfer him to Gladesville Mental Hospital in Sydney. A telegram with the details of the move was sent under cipher to Sydney. His transport was then arranged with a doctor and two armed guards for 6 December. When this telegram was received in

Sydney though, a telephone call was promptly made to the group commandant advising that Naka was not under any circumstances to be sent to Sydney. A number of telegrams and phone calls bounced back and forth between Hay, Sydney and Melbourne regarding Naka's situation. Finally a decision was made to transfer Naka to Gladesville on 11 December. The instructions to Hay emphasised that: 'Lieutenant Naka under strong escort to Mental Hospital Gladesville on Saturday December 11'. Again, the Swiss authorities were advised, with the consulate general acknowledging the advice and noting that arrangements could be made for someone from the consulate to visit Naka if required.

It was a long, arduous and monotonous road trip from Hay to Sydney in 1943 and Naka was handcuffed for the entire journey with an armed escort closely watching. Naka finally arrived and was admitted to Gladesville's Ward 3M on Sunday morning 12 December just after 10 am. Staff observed the fresh cut on his head and two scars on his right leg and another one on his left wrist and noted the details in his new medical record. Although weighing in at only about 100 pounds (48 kg) this was somewhat of an improvement on the skeletal 80 pounds (39 kg) when he was captured 11 months earlier. His temperature was noted as normal but his pulse was slightly elevated at 84. He was then prescribed five grains of calomel as a laxative with his general pallor a concern. As he was thought to be anaemic, he was also prescribed an iron supplement.

* * *

By the end of 1943, the tide was clearly turning and although some of the hardest fighting was yet to come, Australian soldiers generally had a sense that the once invincible Japanese were slowly being beaten. This sense of inevitable and ultimate victory came from not just Australian heroics in the jungles of the South Pacific, but also from the growing awareness of the relentless industrial might, manpower and determination of the United States. That year, Aussie diggers were writing home with a government-issue Christmas card specially printed with the following verse:

There was a young soldier and he
Dreamed of Christmases full of whoopee;
He'd had them before,
And he'll have them some more
When the Japs are where all Japs should be

While not exactly Shakespeare, this rhyme indicated the new levels of confidence about the war that most Australians were now feeling and clearly there was no love lost between the two armies. Yet here in Naka's case was a substantial effort by the Australian authorities, amidst severe domestic shortages and privations, to look after the mental health of one very troublesome Japanese prisoner of war.

Gladesville Hospital was a 'mental asylum' a solid example of the mid-20th century model that used the most modern curative techniques of the day on its patients. Considered counter-productive by today's standards, these procedures largely comprised electric shock combined with intensive drug treatments and isolation. The 'mental asylum' option was often the last alternative used by Australian authorities when they did not know how to handle certain Japanese prisoners.

Naka was a patient, or more accurately, inmate, there from December 1943 until March 1946, eight months after the end of the war. Also interned was Shichijo Shojiro, the prisoner from Cowra who had tried to take a guard's rifle and, following being charged, had become mentally unstable. There were other Japanese patients, one of whom was listed as a 'suspected war criminal'. That some Japanese soldiers, taught to die rather than surrender, would suffer mental health issues after capture, was no surprise and conceivably the suspected war criminal may have been haunted by his past actions.

Naka's records reveal that he was interviewed by a 'Miss James' on two occasions about 12 months apart. The first meeting was on 3 February 1944 where she is mentioned as 'Interpreter, Miss James, Victoria Barracks'. The second visit was on 25 January 1945 where she is acknowledged as 'Miss James, "Intelligence"'. In that appointment she describes Naka as 'suspicious, arrogant, offensive' and 'will be troublesome'. At this time, the hospital records note that he was 'confused', 'hallucinating' and 'hearing voices' that were telling him 'to die or to go home'.

Who was the mysterious 'Miss James'? She may simply have been a well-regarded intelligence officer who spoke fluent Japanese and whose role was simply to obtain information from this young lieutenant. One could picture her as B-grade movie stereotype—approaching middle age, wearing a tweed jacket and skirt, severe, professional and carrying a loaded automatic pistol in her handbag. The only Miss James working at Sydney's Victoria Barracks at the time was officially listed as being employed as a typist. The idea though of sending a typist from 'intelligence' to interview or interrogate a Japanese prisoner simply does not add up.

It is likely that the mysterious Miss James actually worked for the Combined Operational Intelligence Centre (COIC) in Victoria Barracks. Naka had been captured in January 1943 and there would have been little new information that he could provide of any real use, especially in the latter part of the war. The New Guinea campaigns were now in their final phases and the war had moved on. Rather than seeking military intelligence from Naka, it is likely that she was actually engaged in undertaking routine assessments of Japanese prisoners knowing that the war was nearing its end. Her visit may have coincided with the reality of the war coming to a close and the commencement of the administrative processes in compliance with the Geneva Convention to return these men to Japan.

This assumption is contradicted somewhat by the Gladesville Hospital visitor records which note on at least two occasions that she was 'an interpreter'. Miss James also visited the other Japanese Cowra prisoner, Shichijo Shojiro, where it was noted that his normally dull and depressed state 'brightened up' when she spoke to him in Japanese. In 1944, it would have unusual enough for an unmarried woman to have such a relatively senior position in army intelligence, so she must have possessed special skills to interview potentially dangerous prisoners. One obvious skill was her Japanese fluency. The following interpretation of her role has been developed through some unique insights from the Australian Museum of Army Intelligence located at Canungra in Queensland.[24]

Combined Operational Intelligence Centre (COIC) staff duties generally included security in the 'rear areas' or, in military terminology, the 'Lines of Communication'. This was before the creation of the Australian Federal Police or the Australian Security Intelligence Organisation (ASIO). In this period, it fell to the local State police forces, with the assistance of army intelligence personnel, to conduct rear-area security duties. One of the responsibilities of COIC at this time was keeping tabs on prisoners of war whose camps were generally located in more remote areas of Australia. While this remoteness was comforting for urban populations, the security of these prisoners, located close to vital supply dumps, roads and railways was of continuing concern to army intelligence.

Naka then, along with other Japanese prisoners not in regular camps but scattered throughout assorted locations, was not easily monitored by COIC, so someone had to check on him. The explanation, therefore, behind Miss James's visit may be simply that someone at COIC in Victoria Barracks decided to do a headcount of prisoners in NSW and Miss James, a Japanese speaker at COIC, was told to go out to Gladesville and check on both Naka and Shojiro. That the visits to Naka were 12 months apart indicates that the authorities were not too worried about him. Intelligence officers were also allotted to all major prisoner camps to report on their inmates on a regular basis to COIC, so her visits may have simply represented good housekeeping on the part of army intelligence.

* * *

Gladesville staff regularly observed that Naka was commonly suicidal and it was therefore agreed that he should undergo electric shock therapy (ECT). This controversial therapy had only recently been adopted in Australia and was still undergoing adaptations in different locations

24 I am indebted to The Hon Angus Taylor MP and The Hon Kevin Andrews MP who requested Captain Dennis Magennis to undertake research to provide this information.

around the world. ECT was in fact the outcome of a number of medical theories and observations into the effects of convulsions on mental health patients over centuries. The ancient Greek doctor Hippocrates had noted in the fourth century BC that, when malarial fevers induced convulsions in insane patients, some were cured of their mental afflictions. In the Middle Ages, physicians also observed similar effects in mental asylums after a severe fever caused convulsions in patients. The smallpox vaccine of the late 18th century also produced fever and convulsions in mental health patients who were seen to show some improvement. The theory was that, rather than relying on the natural and random occurrence of a disease to produce fever and then convulsions, doctors should be able to induce these convulsions. Investigations into safe methods of triggering convulsions were investigated for decades. These included the use of drugs such as insulin and Metrazol and, later, the non-pharmaceutical approach of ECT. This involved the attaching of electrodes to the head of the patient and running an increasing current through the circuit and into the brain.

Now largely discredited, the typical method of administering ECT to a patient was to use a relaxant such as curare and an anaesthetic to reduce the incidences of fractures in the bones due to severe muscle contraction. Sometimes though, these chemicals were not available and ECT was administered in a basic form. One of the problems with ECT was that some doctors would become addicted to its use. Unfortunately, there were numerous abuses involving repetitive application of ECT up to three times daily to subdue 'troublesome' patients. In Naka's case the limited use of ECT indicates a treatment-based approach rather than a control or punishment procedure. Whatever the motive, it seemed to have little impact on Naka who attempted to escape to commit suicide by climbing up the wire door to get on to the roof of the hospital on 13 August 1945. His records at this point noted that over the period he was at Gladesville he was found to be unsociable and generally self-absorbed. He appeared to improve one day and then deteriorate the next and would suggest that he wanted to either die, go back to Japan, or that the staff were trying to kill him. Electric shock therapy was discontinued, though he was medicated regularly. It was well recognised at this time that when the enemy was losing the war the prisoners' anxiety states increased.

Gaining an understanding of Naka at this time is difficult, though it may indicate some of the pressures he was under. He was in a truly alien environment from any perspective. He was a captured Japanese soldier at a time when the Bushido code demanded that he vanquish his enemies or die in battle. As an officer, he felt guilty because he had survived but had lost all his men. On top of this, he was ill and suffered regular bouts of malaria with at least one recurrence of scabies.

One individual who in 2016 was able to offer a modern-day understanding of Naka's situation is Dr Richard White,[25] a psychiatrist with a deep knowledge of mental health treatments in NSW at the time of Naka's incarceration at Gladesville. White provided, in a considered and compassionate manner, an appreciation of Naka's case and what he might have been experiencing. He did this on the basis that it would be unjust to make an assessment of him that might be untrue, whether Naka was now living or dead. White studied Naka's records and considered that it was difficult for him to judge how mentally disturbed he might have been. Presuming that Naka was genuinely mentally ill, it was also difficult to judge what category of mental illness he had suffered from and the causes and origins of this condition. Dr White suggested that it would have been invaluable to know the extent to which Japanese prisoners exhibited mental disorders while they were prisoners in Australia. Was it common or were these only isolated cases? How often did their situation take the form of guilt and suicidality? Naka had requested on a number of occasions that the guards shoot him and, rather than diminishing over time, his guilt appeared to compound and increase from Brisbane to Cowra to Hay and to Gladesville.

25 Dr Richard White is a Fellow of the Royal Australian and New Zealand College of Psychiatrists and a Member of the Royal College of Psychiatrists (UK) and an AHPRA registered consultant psychiatrist and was a senior staff psychiatrist at the Royal Prince Alfred hospital for over 35 years. He was the director of the psychiatry service at RPAH and, mostly of that period, a clinical senior lecturer at the University of Sydney, where he is now an Honorary Associate of the Discipline of Psychiatry at the Central Clinical School. For a time he was chair of the section for the History, Philosophy and Ethics of Psychiatry of the RANZCP.

CHAPTER 14

While sullen and surly, the Japanese prisoners at Cowra were generally cooperative, but only to the extent that they felt it necessary. Generally, they complied because Japanese 'group think', tribal behaviour, loyalty and dependability are much prized character traits in Japanese society. Soon after capture, they established their 'pecking order'; they organised themselves into social groups; played cards, baseball and sumo wrestling; had a theatrical group and cooked their own food with local rice and fish flown in from New Zealand. The negative effects of incarceration manifested themselves more in cases of disobedience rather than in depression, mental illness and anxiety.

Some questions were posed to Dr White: Could Naka's malaria and its recurrences have contributed to his mental condition? Might some of Naka's behaviour be explained knowing that malaria, even in its mildest forms, has been associated with a number of psychiatric symptoms, including changes in personality and mood, memory, thought patterns and general behaviour? Further, could malaria's effects be complicated somewhat by the complementary psychiatric problems associated with the drugs used to treat malaria? With a paucity of medical records and not knowing the nature of Naka's malaria treatments White considered the possibilities of such a contribution to Naka's mental state. He agreed that such cause and effect could not be ruled out.

White made a general observation that the difficulty in understanding Naka's behaviour is compounded by his abnormal situation. Naka had an Eastern cultural value system and brought his peculiar civilian and military values to an alien Western setting. This unique situation would have been compounded by being both a prisoner of war and inside a mental asylum. The accounts of his aural hallucinations are not helpful to an understanding of his suffering. It is obvious though that he felt terrible guilt, which may at least partially be explained by the strictures of his cultural background, the punitive circumstances of his military service and his shamed status as a prisoner of war. Before he was admitted to Gladesville, he was obviously distressed and would yell out that he had 'snakes in his insides' and could hear the 'voice of God'. Were these hallucinations or misinterpretations of his Japanese utterances? After his admission, there were no more reports of hallucinations during his 27 months in Gladesville Hospital.

* * *

Naka's troubled legacy at the Cowra camp should have resulted in a positive outcome—significantly upgraded security and awareness of the volatile value systems of Japanese prisoners of war. In some ways it did. Increased numbers and types of weapons were provided for the guards but the fences remained at 5–6 feet (150–180 cm) in height. Naka's court martial had provided an insight into the mind of one and maybe many Japanese and his prior escape was proof that the security arrangements were decidedly inadequate. Australian authorities also knew the details of the tragic Featherston, New Zealand, incident in February 1943 when the guards lost control when facing the unyielding intransigence of Japanese prisoners. In Cowra, the Australian authorities had been serendipitously presented with a window of opportunity—a rare chance to better understand the depths of the Japanese psyche. But having heard the sound of an approaching storm, this chance was squandered, despite the pleadings of Cowra's Commandant Monty Brown to his superiors. The Japanese prisoners in B Compound at Cowra were the Kamikaze, the '*Divine Wind*', desperately looking for a reason to regain their honour. That opportunity was now about to be handed to them.

CHAPTER 15

DID WE LEARN NOTHING FROM THIS?

The breakout of 1104 Japanese prisoners from Cowra POW Camp on 5 August 1944 changed this otherwise peaceful country town forever.

The tragic episode in many ways defined the community of Cowra which now hosts a beautifully tended Japanese war cemetery, the only one outside of Japan, and a Japanese Garden and Cultural Centre, Peace Bell and Peace Precinct featuring the prisoner of war campsite; and there is now an enduring friendship between the peoples of the Japanese economic powerhouse and the small town of Cowra.

What would Cowra be like today if there had been no breakout? The short answer is probably like any other mid-size Australian rural community. It would still be picturesque, its tree-lined streets nestled around a stark rock-studded hill of basalt and granite outcrops with the township gently sloping down to the fertile banks of the Lachlan River. It would still be a prosperous and diversified agricultural community with a smattering of secondary industries but it would be without its unique relationship with Japan. And what of Japan? A total of 231 (three more would die in the following months) ex-prisoners, all with their own unique personalities, characters, hopes and demons, would have returned to the burned, bombed rubble of a homeland, but one that had so much promise. Many would seek out families, friends or military colleagues with whom they had experienced and suffered so much. Possibly they would have prayed at shrines to lost kinfolk.

It is hard to see the future from the present, and these men would not have been able to visualise, from the ruins of their imperial empire, the Japanese postwar resurgence. That within 19 years they would host the world at the Olympics Games, and possess the office towers, modern cars and bullet trains would have been inconceivable. These men may well have played their part in that new Japan with families, wives, children and grandchildren, but keeping silent about their memories of a past war and their time at Cowra.

The Cowra Breakout 70th Anniversary in 2014 featured a special guest with something important to say. Japanese ex-prisoner of war Teruo Murakami returned to Cowra and spoke about two subjects. His first was that the Japanese prisoners have never considered the events of August 1944 as a 'breakout' in the true sense of the term. Where were they to escape to? he asked. They knew they had no chance of getting back to their homeland. Also, why would they want to? They all knew and believed that, if they did, they would be immediately executed upon their return.

No, he said, they wanted to riot, to cause as much mayhem as possible, to kill Australian soldiers, and to die so that they could redeem themselves. So, he said, the event should be titled the 'Cowra Riot' or 'Cowra Uprising' but never the 'Cowra Breakout'. During his stay in Cowra, he also visited the poignant memorial that is the Japanese War Cemetery where his mood changed in an instant, becoming angry and restless. Walking slowly and deliberately past each marker, seeing the names of friends and compatriots, he stopped and thrust an arm out, pointing to a name on one bronze plaque that was heavy with the patina of oxidisation. This was the grave of one Yoshio Shimoyama. 'This was the man,' his hand shook and he gestured angrily to the small gathering, 'that drove us to riot.'

The local historians amongst the small group that accompanied Murakami that morning looked at each other in puzzlement. Yes, he was mentioned briefly in Harry Gordon's book but they had not considered him to be one of the serious leaders. 'We have all heard of some who led the breakout: Kanazawa, Kojima, and Minami, but not him.'

'Yes it was him,' Murakami said, agitated. 'It was this man who hid himself behind others,' he said in his disgust at the agitator who was complicit in sending 231 Japanese and five Australians to their deaths.[26] In doing so, in Murakami's eyes and in the eyes of his fellow Japanese prisoners, Shimoyama had committed an unspeakable crime, that of betraying his comrades, and now here he was in the cemetery, not killed by an Australian bullet but dead for another reason. Murakami was now reliving the events and emotions, as fresh in his mind as if he was there on the spot.

While Naka was in Gladesville Hospital, plots, intrigues and tensions were growing daily amongst the prisoners, who were becoming increasingly fragile. Since the war ended, an accepted and agreed sequence of events has developed on what led to the breakout, yet this established chronology oversimplifies what was, in fact, a complex and multifaceted situation.

The accepted timeline of incidents leading up to the bloody revolt customarily starts when Major Robert Ramsay summoned Japanese camp leaders Akira (his real name was Ryo but he will be referred to as Akira) Kanazawa, 'Tadeo Minami' (real name Hajime Toyoshima), Kiyoshi Yamakawa and Maseo Kojima to his office at 2 pm on 4 August 1944. Ramsay advised them that, because of increasing overcrowding at the camp, about 700 Japanese prisoners below the rank of lance-corporal were to be immediately moved to the prisoner of war camp at Hay.

All three forcefully objected to this plan but Ramsay dismissed their protests saying: 'There'll be no arguments; it will take place as ordered.' The three leaders expressed their displeasure and, on taking this message back to the various hut leaders, a decision was made to take a vote amongst all prisoners of war whether they were to break out. Although an escape had apparently been planned for some time, the conventional wisdom is that the transfer announcement by the Australian authorities was the trigger and as a result the attack took place early the next morning. While this simple timeline is the accepted scenario for the events leading up to the breakout, the sequence of events is too linear and, in some important respects, factually incorrect.

26 Four killed in and after the breakout, the fifth was a volunteer defence corps soldier, Sergeant Thomas Hancock, who was accidentally shot by a fellow soldier while on patrol after the breakout.

* * *

The truth is that this event was a long time in the making with a range of contributing factors. Chief amongst these was simply the sum total of fear, anxiety and self-loathing experienced by many of the Japanese prisoners at Cowra. Why, then, were these emotions only acted on as violently as they were at Cowra and not in other camps where those same Japanese had been held? There were certainly plenty of opportunities at these other locations for an 'honourable death' and if individuals were so determined to suicide why did they not take the ample occasions available to them after capture? The reality is that many of these soldiers wanted to survive rather than give their lives for the emperor. Many were simply relieved that their war was over and were now happy to enjoy the relative luxury and safety of Allied camps like Cowra. The Japanese officers, in particular, seemed to be generally missing in action as far as militant and even petty examples of disobedience and defiance were concerned. Except for Naka and one other officer who was later killed in the breakout, the officer class actively avoided any controversy. It appears that the leaders in B Compound even discounted the necessity to keep the officers informed right up to the time of the actual attack even though communications between the two separated compounds was effected on a regular basis by semaphore signalling by the naval prisoners. There was one other circumstance where a flickering electric light due to a faulty connection was thought to be Morse code transmission between the two compounds. When this flashing was observed and the 'code' written down and translated it was found to be gibberish. Some thought it was a complex cypher until the army electrician discovered the problem!

For many of the hardliners at Cowra, this relieved acceptance of defeat was intolerable. The strict hierarchy of the Imperial Japanese forces remained central to the prisoners' life though, with any docility or indifference on the soldiers' part discouraged by regular and severe bashings and beatings that were administered by their non-commissioned officers (NCOs). Also effective were more subtle traditional Japanese methods of control such as ostracism. While individual soldiers may have been thankful to be out of the war, as a group their shame was reinforced daily by these NCOs and exacerbated by the constant arrival of new Japanese prisoners. The question became, in the group conscience of the Japanese, how and when this shame could be obliterated.

There were only a handful of leaders in the power structure of B Compound where the warrant officers and non-commissioned officers were accommodated. These 'honchos', as they were called, were supplemented by the hut leaders who tended to be compliant and supportive. Allied soldiers had often heard Japanese soldiers call their leaders 'honcho' and US soldiers subsequently took the word back to the USA in the 1950s and business leaders became the 'head honcho' and the term is still in use today. The actual Japanese word is 'hancho'.

In the camp hierarchy, the initial leader was a pilot named Tadeo Minami who had crashed in the first raid on Darwin, but he was later deposed by Akira Kanazawa. Leaders and changes of leaders had to be approved by each camp commandant. Minami though was still part of this leaders' group together with another pilot, Maseo Kojima. Others such as Ichijiro Do and Marekuni Takahara were also regularly consulted on important issues. The real hardliner and 'tough guy' appears to have been the Yoshio Shimoyama identified 70 years later by Murakami.

The first arrivals at the Cowra camp were small numbers of prisoners who had been captured in New Guinea from the Allied counter-attack on the Gona, Buna and Sanananda areas in late 1942 and early 1943, with Maseo Naka one of these. While that campaign represented an early reversal for the Japanese, the Allies were still up against a powerful enemy and there would be many battles to go before Japan was considered to be on the back foot. Therefore, those prisoners who arrived in Cowra in early 1943 still considered themselves to be on the winning side. Although they were personally disgraced as POWs, their conduct reflected their being part of a victorious Imperial Japanese Army. As the war progressed and their defeats increased, newly captured Japanese soldiers often saw things quite differently. They had witnessed firsthand the immense firepower of the United States and its seemingly inexhaustible resources and they knew they were now losing the war. Higher command Japanese knew that the New Guinea campaign was a reaction to other events rather than a meticulously planned strategy and campaign and so it was always a gamble which Japan ultimately lost. The attitudes of these new hands with their sober understanding of the real state of affairs caused clashes with the earlier prisoners who still dreamed of victory. Naka was one of those and he could justify in his own mind that he had never surrendered but rather had been captured whilst unconscious. The traditional navy versus army rivalry also resurfaced at Cowra.

While the authorities at Cowra were well aware that the Japanese prisoners were capable of and likely to be planning an uprising, they could only guess when and in what form it might take. News of the Featherston incident in New Zealand in February 1943 had filtered through even to the Japanese and it was likely that some Australian guards gloated about it to bait the prisoners in B Compound.

The first informant in the camp who would trigger the Australians' concern about a possible uprising was a Korean named Takao Matsumoto. Captured in Dutch New Guinea, Matsumoto had taken a Japanese name but was still treated as a second-class person by the Japanese. When Matsumoto and another Korean called Terakawa arrived at Cowra, they were allocated to B Compound. While they had no particular bond as soldiers, they stuck together because the Japanese made it clear that they considered them to be much less than equal to a Japanese.

The Australian interpreter, Manchurian-born Oleg Negerevich, introduced the two to Minami who had been allocated the role of looking after the new arrivals. But they didn't exactly hit it off. Minami was scowling and unpleasant to the two Koreans, although Matsumoto tried his best to fit in. As well as taking a Japanese name, Matsumoto followed the Bushido doctrines he had learnt on the battlefield and had fought and almost lost his life for its principles. He felt no strong allegiance to Japan though and valued his life above dying for the emperor. His aim was to stay alive and to return home. He was also a good listener and a reliable observer—perfect qualities for an informer. He knew the layout of the camp and could filter, sort and correlate information heard as gossip. He began to hear of a potential uprising and saw how this information could impact and assist the Australians' security. A self-starter, he planned to collect as much information as he could and reveal it to the guards on the condition that he would be separated from the Japanese. His long-term strategy was to keep himself safe and get back to Korea after the war.

Matsumoto listened for snippets of information, much of it useless: complaints of hangovers from the crude sake that the prisoners brewed within their huts, reminiscences about wives and girlfriends and talk about baseball. On one occasion though, he overheard a conversation about a proposed attack on the perimeter wire. Weapons were mentioned and an arsenal of knives and clubs had been amassed. It was said to be a plan to escape, attack the camp guards, get their weapons and attack the military camp. The conversation ended with the chilling words: '…we will die in battle.'

The Korean pair then had a stroke of luck. They were to be transferred to D Compound as the camp authorities became aware how the Japanese soldiers were mistreating the Koreans in B Compound. The two were led off by a guard and taken in through the gates from Broadway into their new unit in D Compound. This area was fenced off into three sub-compounds, D1, D2, and D3, with the Koreans and Chinese located together; Japanese officers together; and Italian hardline fascists in another.

Matsumoto found himself located adjacent to A Compound in D1, the Italian area. Internal security was not strongly enforced in this area and, one day, Matsumoto struck up a conversation in broken English with an Italian in A Compound who invited him to cross the inadequate wire barrier between the two compounds and visit his hut. Matsumoto traversed this no-man's-land easily and the Italian showed Matsumoto his hut where they sat down on his bed and looked at girlie magazines, ate chocolate and caught up on news, with Matsumoto offered an English dictionary to study.

This nascent and seemingly innocent friendship was short-lived though, with a guard who seemed to appear from nowhere at the doorway yelling: 'What's going on here?' Matsumoto was arrested, taken away and given 10 days' detention for his troubles. This minor security breach and disciplinary matter was to have important consequences for the security of the camp. While incarcerated, Matsumoto told his guards that he had something important he had to tell an officer.

After his release, Matsumoto was interviewed by intelligence officer Captain Reuben 'Poppa' Mann.[27] This fascinating individual had been a lecturer at the Imperial University in Tokyo before the war. Due to his background, Mann's military area of expertise was intelligence gathering rather than security. For the interview, Matsumoto was brought into the interrogation area with Captain Lord Kane and also Mann. Matsumoto said that he wanted to say something private in Japanese.

He said that 'if something happens, the Koreans would have to suffer too, and that would not be right, because they are not Japanese and will not be involved in any trouble.' He also said, in the typical pleading language often used by powerless prisoners, that he would be called a traitor for what he was about to say.

'What is it that you want to tell us?' asked Mann in Japanese. Matsumoto speaking quietly but insistently announced that there was 'trouble' coming from 'around 700 Japanese' in B Compound and, whilst appearing to be cooperative at the moment, they were planning to escape the camp, attack the garrison, seize weapons and attack the military camp.

This information was immediately reported to Commandant Monty Brown who was reportedly deeply shocked at the news. While stories of a planned uprising were perennial local gossip around the camp and in town, this discovery was the first high-level intelligence that indicated that an attack on the guards was a probability rather than just a distant rumour. Details of the report were conveyed by intelligence staffer, Warrant Officer Lionel Boorman, to the 55-year-old Major Robert Ramsay who dismissed it as a self-serving fabrication

27 This was previously Lt Reuben Mann who had mentored interrogator Alister Kentwell in Queensland.

exclaiming: 'Bloody nonsense, and are you going to believe every Korean who wants to crawl to you?' Boorman would have been well within his rights to take offence at this thinly veiled insult. He was one of the best intelligence men at the camp; a legally trained, no nonsense, and deliberate man who was exasperated when his intelligence reports were overlooked, ignored and disregarded by his superiors. Warrant officers are traditionally entitled to talk back to and critique the decisions of commissioned officers and, as Boorman walked away, he offered a parting remark that he considered the report to be 'valid' and 'important'. He said that, if Ramsay did not want to take any notice of it, then he would own the consequences of that decision. Ramsay, a Military Cross recipient, already bore a significant blemish on his record as he had been caught out some two years before when he was found guilty at a court martial of knowingly falsifying records for paid work for Italian prisoners that was never completed. Questions would later be asked about whether Ramsay, just prior to the breakout, had said certain things to the Japanese leaders and whether he should have passed their response back to his superiors.

Fortunately for Boorman, Monty Brown did take notice and requested an increase in security and armaments for the camp from Sydney. With these resources, Brown intended to seal up B Compound with as much security as possible. Two Vickers machine guns were subsequently installed outside the compound with more hand grenades, submachine guns, and rifles issued to the guards. The officers in charge of each individual compound, including Ramsay, were then ordered to cooperate with each other in the case of an emergency. In any crisis, each compound could call on the others for assistance and also raise the alarm at the Cowra military training camp with a pre-arranged signal of verey lights (flares).

Commanding officer at the 14th Infantry Training Centre on the other side of Cowra was Colonel John Mitchell and he was told of the escape plans on 8 June 1944. He was not particularly pleased by the news and offered the opinion that, while the camp had almost 1700 troops enlisted, most were untrained boys who: 'would not know anything about firing an arrow' let alone a rifle. His comments proved prophetic as the youth and inexperience of his 'men' caused a number of problems during the interminable nine-day round-up of escaped Japanese prisoners.

Meanwhile, prisoner numbers were increasing every couple of weeks with the mounting Japanese defeats. Tensions were also rising in the camp with the Australian intelligence officials warning that the B Compound leaders were 'stirring up' trouble. They advised that the easiest way to overcome this was to transfer the private soldiers away from the camp and the influence of their non-commissioned officers. Brown was also sending increasingly desperate requests to Sydney concerning the overcrowding and requesting that a number of prisoners be moved out. Finally his superiors at Victoria Barracks agreed and Brown then passed on the message to Ramsay that 700 were to be moved forthwith to Hay.

CHAPTER 16

WE CHOOSE TO DIE!

While the decision to transfer the privates had been approved at levels higher than Cowra, achieving this effectively would not be easy. Ramsay had drawn the short straw and, as the officer-in-charge of B Compound, had to complete the task. He and Negerevich discussed how to handle this sensitive operation and the best way to advise the B Compound leader. Negerevich thought that the best way to do this was to make another of his normal visits to the Japanese compound but this time he would make a special effort to look and listen to assess the mood. He reported back to Ramsay that the prisoners seemed fairly oblivious to anything that might be going to happen. This was in spite of the fact that, in an unfortunate piece of administrative timing, the prisoners had just been informed that, due to general shortages, their cigarette ration was being cut from 35 cigarettes per prisoner per week to only 21 per week. Most of the Japanese were heavy smokers and one can only speculate whether the reduction in nicotine may have resulted in increased agitation within the compound at this critical time.

Ramsay summoned Kanazawa, Minami, Yamakawa and Kojima and gave them the bad news[28]. How and what was said during this fatal conversation has been subsequently disputed. Ramsay testified at the official inquiry that he categorically informed the four that 700 Japanese below the rank of lance-corporal were being transferred to the camp at Hay. In his book *Voyage from Shame*, Harry Gordon stated that in 1977 Kanazawa told him that Ramsay never advised them of the removal by rank. Gordon also stated that when he spoke to Negerevich many years later, he corroborated Kanazawa's statement, saying: "We knew that, if we had told them about separation by rank, it would have caused a blow-up so we avoided that completely."

28 Only Kanazawa and Yamakawa would survive the breakout.

Did Kanazawa, Negerevich and Ramsay all have recall problems? In later years Kanazawa spoke highly of Ramsay saying that there was a good level of mutual respect and that he considered the Japanese had always been treated fairly. There does not appear to be any real reason that Negerevich would side with the Japanese version of events in opposition to Ramsay. However, something is not quite right with these earlier statements and recollections and we need to take a little break and look at what occurred.

From 24 to 26 January 1945, the murder trial of Akira Kanazawa was held in the YMCA building at the Cowra camp. Kanazawa, at age 28, unlike many of the other prisoners was a professional soldier, a twice-decorated sergeant-major in an engineering regiment. He had served in China as well as the South Pacific and bore the scars of two gunshot wounds. Captured at Tufi near Cape Nelson in New Guinea relatively early in April 1943, he, like others at that time, still considered himself to be part of the "winning team". Though small in stature at just 5 feet 3 inches (160 cm) he was nevertheless a commanding presence and had taken over from Tadeo Minami as leader of B Compound. Kanazawa would face two trials on two separate charges, the first being the murder of Private Benjamin Gower Hardy, one of the Vickers machine gunners. The second was conspiring with Hiroshi Yoshida and other Japanese prisoners to break out of the camp in a body of "force and violence." Kanazawa was charged with murder on the basis of the English law principle that a person promoting and instigating a crime, while not responsible for the physical act of murder, is nevertheless guilty of it. Bringing a charge of the murder of Private Hardy only and not Ralph Jones, his No. 2 on the Vickers gun, was a technical matter and while the murder was a civil offence the trial was conducted by a military court. It was pointed out on a number of occasions that while Kanazawa did not actually commit the assault on Hardy, he was nevertheless culpable as the recognised leader of the breakout. The judge advocate cited a hypothetical situation where a trade union group was demonstrating in a public place and a policeman was killed. One union member is arrested and charged with his death. He pointed out that, on the basis of the principle that was proposed, that man if found guilty could hang. Ultimately the judge advocate struck the principle out on the basis of an example which he said if applied in Australia to extreme events would be a very great danger to the liberty "of our own subjects".

This action by the judge advocate all but settled the matter of a murder conviction. It showed that the outcome of the trial was not prejudged in any way but the resultant verdict was likely a surprise to many present. Is it reasonable to suggest that in the back of the judge advocate's mind was the fate of 22,000 Australian POW?

Kanazawa spent a considerable amount of time at his trial setting out that the intent of the uprising was not to attack and kill. They had planned to advance towards the wire into the secure area where they would provoke the Australians to shoot them. They wanted to die so their actions were designed to initiate a violent response from the guards to kill them. The prosecution did not accept this line at all and argued 'Why was it then that you armed yourselves with baseball bats and knives and other offensive weapons and as a result killed three Australians?' Kanazawa was lucky to escape the more serious charge and, while found not guilty of murder, was later found guilty of the lesser charge of conspiracy to riot and was sentenced to 18 months' hard labour. He would serve only 13 of these as he was returned to Japan with the bulk of all Japanese POW in March 1946.

During the murder trial it was clear from the evidence and statements made by Ramsay, Negerevich and Kanazawa that a printed roll of all the Japanese to be moved to the camp at Hay was provided to all four leaders. Under oath Ramsay stated so, as did Negerevich and Kanazawa, thereby dispelling the myth that the Japanese were not told!

But in spite of the above it appears that at the time, there was considerable confusion about who was going and why. It is a reasonable assumption that the Japanese in B Compound had an intelligence network equal to that of the Australians. In reviewing the tragedy at Cowra, time and time again it appears that the Australians were on the back foot in anticipating events. It is likely that the guards throughout the ranks, bored and looking for any diversion, could not help themselves and openly discussed vital information with each other not realising that it was being heard by the Japanese, many of whom spoke English but pretended otherwise.

Intelligent and cunning prisoners are easily motivated and have plenty of time to collate information and form plans. In truth the decision to relocate the Japanese to Hay was a botched operation, pure and simple. On the basis that the two principal concerns for those administering a prisoner of war camp are 'security' and 'keeping the peace', it is incredible that a central issue of overcrowding was handled so poorly. Surviving Japanese prisoners, too many to dismiss, have since advised that, if there had there been meaningful consultation, the tragedy at Cowra would not have occurred. While the Japanese prisoners were often difficult and obstinate to deal with, they were open to reasoned discussions about relevant issues if they felt they were being listened to. These Japanese were also aware of the overcrowding and may well have been receptive to a proposed solution, perhaps on the basis of the prisoners suggesting which groups or individuals might want to go to Hay. While a few did, the general Australian inability to understand the Japanese mind, individually and as a group, was a fatal flaw. This is despite the fact that, after almost three years of intelligence-gathering, there was considerable understanding of how the Japanese thought and operated and how they could be manipulated through both strong discipline and subtlety. Intelligence reports, interrogations, publications on the Japanese, the early experience with Featherston, and Naka's escape, divisive actions and court-martial, should all have been considered when making the unilateral decision to transfer the Japanese lower ranks to Hay. While risk management is a critical component of doing business in the 21st century this concept was less understood in the 1940s. At the Cowra camp in August 1944, the risks of the transfer decision were high but any effort in reducing them appears to have been lacking as a deliberate and considered process. If the definition of an accident is an unsafe action in an unsafe situation the 'situation' at the Cowra camp on that day was a classic example of it. There was no intention by the Australians to stir up trouble nevertheless that was the result.

CHAPTER 16

Now let us return to 4 August 1944. After being told of the transfer, Kanazawa, Minami, Yamakawa and Kojima returned to B Compound disoriented, confused and angry. Kanazawa wanted confirmation and sought out Negerevich. Kanazawa was never impressed with Negerevich's ability with the Japanese language but nevertheless they spoke often: 'Is it true that only private soldiers will be going to Hay?'

'Yes,' confirmed Negerevich.

'Please ask the major to reconsider.'

'The orders have already been given and they cannot be changed.'

'We need to reconsider then and have further discussions whether NCOs can go too.'

'It's no use; it is just going to be the privates that are going,' Negerevich confirmed.

Much has been made of the relationship between the Japanese non-commissioned officers and the private soldiers. The view, promoted by the Japanese at the time, that their soldiers were a family, with brothers that needed to be together, was largely a romanticised fantasy. If it was a family, it was a dysfunctional and abusive one where private soldiers were regularly ill-treated by NCOs from lance-corporal up. Physical and mental punishment and mistreatment was not just an occasional event, but was both structured and formalised as well as capricious and erratic. The 'concern' by the camp leaders about the 'non-comms' not going to Hay may simply have been about loss of control once these private soldiers, generally less fanatical, were out of their sight. In reality those on the roll as a 'private' may have been anything but. In later life Kanazawa said that not only had many of the Japanese used false names but also false ranks. In that roll of names were corporals, sergeants and warrant officers!

Negerevich recognised the tension, but again stressed that nothing the camp leaders said was going to change the order. He looked directly at Kanazawa: 'You need to prepare yourself and get ready.' Kanazawa was indeed getting ready, but not for the outcome that Negerevich was talking about. Kanazawa, Minami and Kojima met once more: 'We should contact the officers in D Compound.'

'No,' said Kanazawa: 'They will know soon enough when we reach them when we attack into Broadway.'

Doubts existed about the likelihood of the success of the breakout with the three, and Kojima in particular, believing that the garrison itself could not be overrun, let alone the distant military camp. 'It will just be a way to die,' they agreed. In spite of misgivings about the venture, the ideal of a 'good way to die' was agreed upon. The hardliner Shimoyama then became vocal at this point and urged them on: 'You are Japanese soldiers who need to regain your honour in Bushido spirit!' He also pushed for the attack to occur that night saying that, because the Australians 'love their weekends' and would be relaxed, no extra guards would be on duty with the machines guns left idle. The Australians were indeed relaxed, and it was mostly because they thought that the departure of 700 Japanese prisoners was the solution to the growing tension in B Compound.

Kanazawa sent the word out for the hut leaders to meet with him. He prepared a list of 47 militants that he considered would be good organisers for the planned attack. A little later, the 21 hut leaders filed into Hut 15 for the fatal conference which went for about an hour. The idea of the uprising was discussed and supported, but it was felt that a majority of prisoners would be needed to support the suicidal attack. Surely this increased movement of individuals within B Compound was observed by the guards and, if it was reported, why was it not followed up?

Each leader returned to their respective hut and ballots were held, with each prisoner voting on a piece of toilet paper which they could mark with a cross (to not break out) or a circle (to break out). The leaders gathered the votes and headed off to give Kanazawa the news; 80 per cent were in favour of the attack. An excited and exuberant Shimoyama raced into Hut 15, loudly proclaiming: 'My men want to go and are ready to die.'

Kanazawa considered that he had successfully picked the general mood of the hut leaders as well as his 47 advisors and now felt pressured to accept the result of the ballot. When, at his murder trial, the defending officer asked him what the decision was he stated: 'There were about 1085 POW in camp because some were in hospital. Almost unanimously they decided to die irrespective of what the order was. That was transmitted to Major Ramsay.' Here is a key and astounding point to this whole matter: if it was true that Ramsay was told of the decision by the Japanese prisoners of war 'to die', it should have reverberated to the top and led to an emergency situation. Considering what had happened at Featherston in 1943 and Camp Paita in January 1944 should this statement not have caused serious alarm at the camp? That this statement about Ramsay being told was not followed up with further questioning at the trial is equally incredible.

As far as the ballot is concerned there is significant evidence to suggest that the result had been falsified and that the actual count was changed between the time of the actual voting and when the result was delivered to Kanazawa. While this is anecdotal from former prisoners with their recollections well after the war, the belief that the vote was rigged is widespread and enough to cast doubt on the real level of support from all the prisoners. Survivors of the breakout hold definite views on this life-and-death decision and how it was determined. Some said they were coerced in their voting; others said many huts were defiantly against the breakout; and others said that their votes were never even collected. As the hut leaders were mostly hardline traditionalist navy men, it is possible that many of them reported what they thought was expected of them.

One ex-prisoner also said they were all in a highly excited and peculiar mental state that day due to the rising tension. Many of the prisoners who survived later said that they were against the uprising. The 'navy group' were in the ascendency at that time but had to maintain and keep increasing the pressure on those around them to retain their power.

In this particular situation, a unique aspect of Japanese culture came to the fore and became probably the most influential aspect of the whole affair. This effect is known as *Amae no Kouzou* (system of indulgence) and displayed a typical Japanese characteristic shown in the ballot result. The system acknowledges and accepts human fallibility, thereby permitting individuals to behave illogically and irrationally. This meant that, despite the forlorn nature of their venture, the militaristic culture in which they had all been raised now dictated what would happen at Cowra that day. In reality, the vote appears to have been a sham. While purporting to be an exercise in soldierly brotherhood deciding together what was to be done, it was instead cynically manipulated by the hardliners to get the result they had always intended. They then forced this falsified vote onto Kanazawa who felt compelled to make the announcement that: 'We will all break out!' The order now given was taken back to each hut and all were compelled to obey. Interestingly but not all that surprisingly, after the breakout it was discovered that a number of the hardliners had survived the ferocious machine gun and rifle fire, whereas many of the reluctant ordinary soldiers were lying dead after following orders.

One prisoner who did not want to die was Warrant Officer Shichibei Matsushima. A moody, morose and temperamental prisoner, he dreamed only of getting back to Japan to his beloved wife and children. After hearing of the proposed breakout, he hatched his own plans to let the Australians know that an attack was imminent. He wrote notes on pieces of paper under assumed identities naming himself as a troublemaker who needed to be removed. He threw these into Broadway hoping for them to be picked up by a guard so that he would be arrested, taken away, and interrogated where he could reveal the attack. The notes were not picked up until three days after the breakout, by which time hundreds of Japanese prisoners and five Australians lay dead! Matsushima's treachery was not discovered and he survived, later to return to Japan.

Private Alfred Rolls drew duty that night and he remembered it as being 'bloody cold'. He was stationed in the middle of Broadway, relentlessly pursued by an icy wind that blew from across the surrounding paddocks and whistled around his ears. A small canvas tent, a standard wooden office chair to sit on and a telephone connected to the guard house, were his only companions that cold moonlit night. To keep the circulation going in his 40-year-old feet, he would walk incessantly up and down his patrol area, stamping on the hardpacked dirt surface to stay warm. Cold as he was, he made sure not to move too far from his post. Around 1.30 am, the wind died down and it wasn't as cold. At about 1.45 am he saw what looked like a figure bobbing around in the dark between the buildings in B Compound. The figure became clearer and was now running towards the barbed wire trying to get Rolls's attention. This unidentified Japanese had cracked under the strain and was trying to warn the guards. Rolls could not understand the prisoner's broken English but knew by his frantic state that he was saying something of great seriousness so he raised his rifle and fired two shots, the prearranged alarm signal for the camp. He then ran to his telephone to call the guard house. When they asked what was happening, Rolls responded: 'There's a Jap here and he is trying to say something. He's very agitated but I can't make out anything.' But the Japanese were now aware that they had lost the advantage of surprise.

In his hut some 200 metres away, coup leader Minami was interrupted in his thoughts by one of his men saying: 'Minami-san, there's an informer at the wire!'

'Get him,' he ordered and a dozen Japanese instantly sprang out of the hut, but not before the informer had gone over the fence into Broadway. The uprising shattered the morning quiet with more than 1,000 prisoners pouring and screaming out of their huts in swarms, each group with a strategic objective. One group rushed north in a suicidal attack on the machine guns, another group sprinted east to escape into the countryside and then swung around to attack the garrison, with the last group racing into Broadway, splitting to race to the northern and southern gates. One band in Broadway could see the informer running ahead of them and they were not going to let him go. He was soon knocked down after being tackled, clubbed by the improvised bats embedded with nails brandished by the prisoners, his throat cut in an instant and his lifeless body then kicked into a drain.

Rolls was running for his life, knowing full well that they would kill him if they caught him. With his middle-aged lungs burning and his heart pounding he could not work out why no one was firing. Where was the bloody Bren gun that should have been pouring fire into the Japs behind him? The gap was closing but he finally made it to the gate. Some guards had it open and he was through and safe with it securely bolted behind him. Seconds later the rampaging mob were there attacking the gates but rifle fire from A and B Company guards cut them down. Now 18 of the 21 sleeping huts were ablaze and the dry hardwood timber and asbestos roofs crackled like their own volleys of gunfire. Other prisoners headed east; this was the cohort that would suffer the least casualties. There was 'F Tower' and the Japanese had quickly worked out by its field of fire exactly where the protected areas were. The guard up top had an Owen submachine gun but quickly expended his few clips. He had grenades but could not extend his throwing arm back far enough in the confined space for them to be thrown any distance. Breakout hothead Yoshio Shimoyama was running with this group and committed an act of brutality that even the hardened Japanese soldiers couldn't forget. It would be his undoing. He had deliberately stopped when he found a badly wounded countryman lying at his feet and, taking out an improvised knife, unhesitatingly stabbed him in the throat, killing him.[29] A number of the prisoners who witnessed this wanton cruelty then committed it to memory for later reference. The company that headed north towards the Vickers machine guns now faced a murderous crossfire of .303 bullets from two guns. The Japanese that were killed here provided a mound of dead bodies over which their comrades now breached the low fences with a group of four attacking machine gunners Privates Ralph Jones and Ben Hardy.

The gunners had been trained to quickly man the Vickers machine gun in an emergency. When the alarm was sounded by Rolls, two teams of two men raced to each of the guns that were mounted on separate trailers. They were experienced soldiers and knew their jobs; a trained gunner could get his weapon into action in five seconds or less. Normally, a Vickers gun team consisted of six men. Hardy was the No. 1 on the gun (the one who was firing); Jones was the No. 2. There should have also been a No. 3, whose job it was to maintain the 'immediate use' ammunition. Another three men were normally allocated to bring up the replacement ammunition, load the belts if necessary, and provide protection for the gun. As the men numbered three, four, five and six were running towards Hardy and Jones to help, an officer intervened

29 In spite of assurances that knives and metal cutlery supplied to B Compound were counted and collected after use, they never were and provided many weapons for the breakout.

and sent them to assist a Lewis gun instead—a fatal error. This meant that Hardy and Jones were now well and truly on their own. They managed to swing their gun into action but it was only a short time before they would be overwhelmed by the frenzied Japanese and killed.

While their gun was in action they could see what was coming towards them and they knew it was the end! Hardy was about to carry out the drill to make the gun inoperable as per their training. They likely looked at each other in their last moments and said 'disable', knowing the consequences of the gun falling into Japanese hands. They could have easily saved their lives and abandoned the gun but chose to stay, proving themselves to be brave soldiers indeed.[30] They stopped firing even though there was still ammunition left in the belt. In this short time, they had fired just 85 rounds. Hardy then lifted the feed cover and removed the feed block ensuring that the weapon could not be activated by the Japanese who were now jumping onto the trailer. Hardy and Jones had no small arms to defend themselves and were soon overwhelmed—stabbed and clubbed. Jones managed to break free with stab wounds to his chest and back. He ran towards the other gun, managed a couple of words, and fell dead. Now in the trailer, the Japanese had swung the Vickers around intending to take out the other Vickers gunners and then fire into the B Company area but Hardy had done his job well. The feed block now hung off the ammunition belt and, while a trained gunner could insert it quickly and get the gun firing, the prisoners did not know how to do it and while they kept trying, guards advanced and killed them with multiple rifle shots. While this hell was breaking loose around them, Privates Stanley and Yum kept firing from the other adjacent Vickers and, finally, the attack on the northern wire was over.

At the same time on the northern end of Broadway, guards from A and B Compounds were firing rifles and a Bren gun at will into the Japanese rushing towards the gate. In an instant, three of the Australians had gunshot wounds from 'friendly' fire from the other end of Broadway. The injured men were carried off into huts as the Japanese continued to assault the gate despite heavy gunfire. One determined

30 Both were awarded a posthumous George Cross, the non-war-zone equivalent of the Victoria Cross.

Japanese managed to scale the gate with a knife and a club in hand. He broke through the lines running past guard Wal Mackenzie who would later praise the Japanese as fearless and incredibly brave. The solitary prisoner ran past the guards towards the B Company buildings and targeted Private Charles Shepherd who he stabbed in the heart, killing him instantly. Major Ramsay saw it and reacted immediately, ordering one of his soldiers to shoot the prisoner. Both the Japanese and Shepherd lay dead within a few yards of each other.

At the other end of Broadway, the southern cluster of prisoners was trying to link up with the officers in D Compound. One officer, Doctor Ichiro Fujita, saw the commotion and moved out to meet the surge coming towards him. Corporal Don Angwin, a skilled marksman brought in from the military training camp, lined up his Lee Enfield on the Japanese doctor officer.[31] The bullet slammed into both thighs and the doctor bled to death where he fell. Strangely, his death record shows 'Killed during mass escape'; however, the next entry was subsequently altered from 'Gun Shot Wound both legs' to show 'Self-inflicted Wound' as the cause of his demise.

The whole bloody episode was all over in just 30 minutes. After this time, nervous guards 'standing to' would occasionally shoot into B Compound and Broadway at any movement. While Naka was sleeping in his ward at Gladesville Mental Asylum, 300 Japanese were now roaming lost and disoriented in the Cowra countryside. About a dozen of these would commit suicide by hanging or throwing themselves under moving trains. Another group of eight or so would ambush and kill Lieutenant Harry Doncaster who had been abandoned by the young recruits he had been leading. One of their dropped bayonets was used to kill him. The last Japanese escapee was picked up exactly nine days later.

There was one more bloodstained footnote to the tragedy. Breakout ringleader Yoshio Shimoyama, who had slit the wounded Japanese prisoner's throat, was one of those who was recaptured. On his return to B Compound, he was confronted by the surviving prisoners about what he had done. 'Why did you kill Matsumura? He did not asked to

31 See James Henderson's book on Don Angwin, *The Official Secrets Act—Death of a Good Soldier.*

be killed,' they shouted. Under the Japanese code of honour, captured soldiers were to choose death, but this was a decision they had to make themselves. Shimoyama had broken this sacred code by making that decision himself. He had in fact committed murder and was about to pay the price. His crime could have been overlooked under other circumstances, but he had escaped the camp and not died, as he insisted others do, and had returned back unscathed. They had not forgotten and he was in deep trouble. On Wednesday, 9 August, a small group of prisoners was seen moving towards the wire at Broadway where they deposited a body. It was Shimoyama. On the previous evening after a summary trial, a lynching party had appeared where he was sleeping, overwhelmed him, dragged him along the floor, and tied his hands behind his back. A rope was placed around his neck and then thrown over a rafter. As he was being hauled up someone said: 'You should have done this yourself.' His record card stated incorrectly that he had died on 5 August: 'Died: Suicide, strangulation by hanging.' There was no doubt that this was a murder, pure and simple, but it was also clear that the Australians had had enough of their Japanese charges. They wanted the whole thing to go away and with the end of the war in view to have them out of the country as soon as possible. There was little interest in pursuing an alleged murder. It appears that as a result of this incident and a number of others that the authorities were not beyond altering the odd record to suit their purposes.

Shimoyama was buried that day in haste. Lieutenant Colonel Athol Earle Brown (not Monty Brown, the commandant of the camp) was the NSW Director of War Graves and was still in Cowra finalising the proper burial of the hundreds who had died during the breakout. He discovered that Shimoyama had been buried without being viewed by the coroner. Brown arranged for the grave to be reopened and for an inspection to be made by the Coroner Fred Arnold and the Government Medical Officer, local doctor, James Garner. Shimoyama was therefore one of the last prisoners of war to be buried, as befitting one who had played such an ignoble part in the slaughter of the breakout. Having urged others to run to their deaths he would survive as many of the hardliners did, only to be killed by his own kind.

WE CHOOSE TO DIE!

On 18th September 1944, Brigadier William Simpson of the Commonwealth's Security Service, received a letter marked "Secret and Personal". Attached to it was an extract from a Japanese radio broadcast on 10th September 1944, attacking the veracity of Australia's report on the Breakout at Cowra. Simpson was advised that the broadcast should be brought to the notice of the Protecting Power in Sydney - the Swiss Consulate, which was the International Red Cross representative in Australia. It was strongly suggested that the statement should be properly denied and that the true facts should be given world publicity in view of the possible repercussions on our prisoners of war in Japanese hands.

The extract provided to Simpson was as follows (including typographic and punctuation errors) and its contents could hardly have been a surprise. It provides a complete validation of both Japan's official attitude to capture and its duplicity in regard to its stated good treatment of Allied prisoners of war.

"WHAT IS THE TRUE STORY OF THIS AUSTRALIAN PRISON CAMP MURDER?"

Bursting with indignation at the cold blooded murder of Japanese civilian internees, the Nippon people demand to know the true story of the midnight murder of more than 200 innocent Japanese, which Prime Minister John Curtin belatedly reported more than a month after the incident occurred. (Note: Mr. Curtin's statement quotes fully and accurately.) It is perfectly clear to the Japanese people that these unfortunate Japanese were who were murdered in the prison camp, cannot have been prisoners of war, as John Curtin dishonestly claimed; they were internees, for it is a well known fact and accepted fact that the Japanese soldier never permits himself to be taken prisoner. His military creed is that death by his own hand is preferable to the dishonour and humiliation of capture by the enemy. Curtin may not care to admit it but the fact is perfectly obvious that the unfortunate victims of the midnight mass murder were internees, who had lived in Australia for long years before the war. They had become more or less accustomed to the Australian way of living and had a lot in common with Australians, probably they had Australian (friends) and girlfriends. Then, why should they uprise without cause, regardless of the obvious futility of such an attempt? So far, since their internment in 1941, these Japanese had accepted the situation of life as internees, despite the humiliations to which they must have been subjected and the coarseness of life in camp. The Japanese are patient, orderly, well-mannered people provoked by brutality and injustice to such action?.

Curtin, in his report of this horrible story, makes every possible excuse for the outrageous action of those responsible for the welfare of the internees. We would very much like to hear the Japanese version. (Note: Anti-Axis statesmen often alleged atrocities committed by Japan against American, Australian and British POW, as e.g. Cordell Hull, Eden, Curtin; but their information was by no means reliable and no third-party, as e.g. the Vatican or the International Red Cross supported their story. On the contrary Paul Morella, Dr. Pallavicini and Max Pestalozzi repeatedly praised Japanese treatment of POW. It is significant that the Netherlands government, whose nationals constitute a great part of the POW in Japan refused to make such allegations). Curtin's statement on the event came a month after it had happened, Australia obviously has much to hide. Curtin stated that the International Red Cross and representatives of the Protecting Power were free to investigate the matter. Then why has there been no statement by the Vatican authorities or by Protecting Power or the International Red Cross regarding this midnight mass murder? It should be obvious that they have been prevented making a thorough investigation. We appeal to Archbishop Gilroy of Sydney, who has repeatedly deplored and anti-Axis brutality, to insist on a thorough investigation of this matter.

In response, the Red Cross report subsequently forwarded to Tokyo exposed such nonsense!

CHAPTER 17
HOME

The war was over. On 1 March 1946, the *Sydney Morning Herald* reported that a ragged group of Japanese prisoners travelling home on the steamer *Daikai Maru* would be having a 'most unpleasant' voyage. The Japanese-flagged ship had been escorted into Sydney Harbour by two British submarines, the *Tireless* and the *Truncheon.* The Japanese crew of 40 had been checked by Australian security and fingerprinted. They were then given strict orders as to what they could and could not do while on shore leave. The vessel of only 6800 tons was going to have a total of 2800 passengers crammed between decks in three or four holds with the voyage to Japan taking about one month. As befitting the times, it would be no luxury cruise, with four former prisoners to share a space designed for two; their bunks would be fibre mats only about 2 inches (50 mm) thick. The article in the *Herald* stated that: 'the ship emitted an indescribable stench which no breeze could dissipate.' The only bathing facilities were washbasins with no other amenities. The master of the ship was a Captain Riichi Yoshizawa, 54 years old, who had been a naval reservist before the war. Interviewed by the *Herald*, he expressed amazement at the lack of damage around Sydney Harbour. He had been told that Japanese bombers, along with midget submarines, had inflicted considerable destruction, but none was to be seen. Two trainloads of Japanese from Hay and Cowra delivered their prisoners directly to the Sydney docks. Thirty-two prisoners from Cowra were held back as suspected war criminals and would later board a separate ship, the *Katoomba*, and sail to New Britain. Here they would be further investigated for prosecution under the war crimes trials to be held in Rabaul.

Returning Australian prisoners of war took a more than academic interest in these minor trials because etched in their minds were the locations of their captivity and the particular names of cruel Japanese and Korean perpetrators. Australia's position in seeking justice was understandable. As a small nation of around seven million, a total of 22,376 soldiers, nurses and civilians had been held by the Japanese as prisoners. Some 8031 of this number died (fully 36 per cent, or more than one in three) largely through cruelty, disease, neglect, and some even by summary execution. This death toll also represented about 20 per cent of Australia's total World War II casualties!

Nothing further though is known of the 32 prisoners from Cowra and, while their names can be found at the National Archives Australia, they do not appear on any further records for trials prosecuted at Rabaul. It can then be assumed that they were released and ultimately allowed to return to Japan. This does not mean that they were innocent of war crimes. Either the evidence against them was considered inadequate or the Commonwealth Government was not able to justify further expense over the £4 million that had already been spent. The trials were increasingly becoming a public issue; the war had ended and most Australians were now more interested in rebuilding their lives than in the brutalities perpetrated by low-ranking and obscure former Japanese soldiers. More significantly, the USA was pressuring Australia to get them finished and quickly; it was time for everyone to move on.

Like the other prisoners, Maseo Naka was also going home. Transferred from Gladesville Hospital, he was a special case and was taken directly by motor vehicle to the Balmain dock area. Two days later, after taking on supplies and some additional and rather reluctant Chinese internees, the *Daikai Maru* left Sydney and sailed for Japan. Those Formosan-Chinese faced an uncertain future because while they may have been press-ganged into serving with the Japanese forces, many were quite happy to do so. Either way they were collaborators. Some were even members of the feared Black Dragon Society which had emerged at Cowra and which was responsible for at least two murders and a number of assaults inside the camp. Word of their crimes would certainly find their way back to Formosa.

When Naka boarded the *Daikai Maru*, still cursed by anxieties, and paranoias, he was entering a new world and the gateway to a different postwar Japan. There was to be no warm farewell for him such as was being offered by Cowra's Major Robert Ramsay to prisoners of war leader Akira Kanazawa on the wharf that morning. Ramsay and Kanazawa were not friends but, rather, respectful acquaintances, as they were both old soldiers. Kanazawa was a key figure in the breakout at Cowra and had been charged and then acquitted of murder. He may well have been a pawn and an instrument of others, but it was he who bore the wrath of the Australians after the event. On the wharf that morning, Ramsay presented Kanazawa with a watch. Could this have been the first token of reconciliation between two former bitter enemies or was it simply a gift of a watch to a man who had arrived at Cowra without one?

Naka was alone in every sense of the word. He was now not even on the receiving end of the jeers, cheers and taunts from the children and adults gathered at the wharf; he was a non-person. He had in a short time achieved a measure of distinction by being the first Japanese to escape from custody and he had also caused the Australian authorities more trouble than any other prisoner. But now he was just another dishonoured ex-soldier, wondering what future lay in wait for him in Japan. He had spent over two years in Sydney and he knew something that the other Japanese arriving from Cowra and Hay did not: that Japan had largely failed in its efforts to attack and destroy Sydney. Apart from the 30 merchant ships sunk off the east coast of Australia by both Japanese and German submarines, Sydney had suffered just one real attack in 1942 by midget submarines, being largely spared further punishment. It was, as Captain Yoshizawa had said, the promised destruction by Japan of their enemies had proved illusory.

After two years of drug treatment and electro-convulsive therapy, Naka's file was marked with a final, desultory entry: 'not improved'. He had boarded the ship that morning still a deeply troubled soul. Although he was a conscript, he had been in the elite 41st Infantry Regiment and was blooded in battle against some of the best fighting forces in the world: British, Indian, and Australian troops in Malaya and Singapore, and indigenous and American forces in the Philippines. While fighting at Kokoda, he had experienced victories but then the annihilation of his platoon and capture! He, like many other soldiers, had expected that Japan would win the war but now saw only the ignominy that awaited him. Thrust to the lowest rungs of society and perhaps even execution by his own people when he set foot on Japanese soil, he could not know what the future held. There were certainly hardships for these ex-prisoners and the six million other Japanese who would eventually return home from the war. But they could not have any idea how the Allies, led by General Douglas MacArthur, would set about transforming Japan from an imperialist feudal society controlled by opportunistic militarists into a modern civilisation that would soon join the rest of the democratic world to become a truly remarkable nation.

Yet this glittering new society was all in the future. America's legendary news magazine, the *Saturday Evening Post,* ran a forthright and frank article by journalist Harold Noble in October 1946 headed 'The Japs Hate their Heroes'. Noble expressed sympathy for these ordinary Japanese soldiers still returning to their homeland. He painted a bleak landscape, a grey, defeated and damaged Japan facing an unclear future in the shadow of its ever-present conqueror. While most of the returning Japanese showed all the signs of resignation and defeat, many were also relieved as they had been overseas for up to eight years and were now finally home.

Noble witnessed the trickle of tatty uniformed men, bent under heavy travel-stained, weather-beaten packs shuffling out of Shinagawa Railway Station in Tokyo. They stepped hesitatingly out of the crowds, looking up and down the street, uncertain and bewildered, before wandering off in twos and threes to find their way to their homes, if they still existed. Noble called them 'Japan's heroes'; they were back from the war but no one even seemed to notice them or called out 'Welcome home'. Only a few years before, they had been cheered off to victory with marching bands, banners and crowds roaring 'Banzai!' Now nobody cared.

When interviewed, many of these ex-soldiers believed that their own units could have carried on indefinitely in China but, with the Americans landing on Okinawa, they knew Japan was beaten and that it was only a matter of time before the mainland was invaded … and then came 'the bomb'. These returning soldiers, like many of those who had been captured during the long war, were both impressed and troubled by the decency and consideration offered by the Allies to their defeated enemy. They were surprised and disturbed as those acts of compassion showed that they had been told lies by their superiors. But what else was a lie? Noble interviewed one old soldier torn by such mixed emotions over his homecoming that he didn't know how he felt. Naturally, he was happy to be alive and home but so much had happened. The city was so different, the future seemed so dark, and now there was a sudden and overwhelming memory of lost comrades. His unit had left Shinagawa Station all those years ago with 240 fine fellows but only 88 had survived. Here he was now at that same station, just one out of the four million Japanese diaspora who had returned in one of the great migrations in history.

By the end of hostilities in September 1945, about six million Japanese military personnel were scattered over the Pacific and Asiatic mainland. Of these six million, 1.5 million were being held prisoner by the Soviet Union and, with its new postwar isolation and lack of cooperation, little was known of these thousands except that they were detained in the wastelands of Siberia. The rest could be brought home, but how and when? Many thought it would take four or five years to achieve, others up to 10. The countries that still held Japanese military personnel (as far as the Allies were concerned, this also included the Koreans and Chinese who had aligned with the Japanese) wanted them out as soon as possible as they were a drain on limited postwar resources, particularly food supplies. Their repatriation also meant that Japan would now face the same issue. The Japanese could not bring them back, so it would now be up to the Allies, with that task falling mainly to the United States.

This operation to return the Japanese military and civilian personnel to Japan was tasked to a new corporation called SCAJAP (Shipping Control Authority for Japan). This organisation became the largest single shipping agency in the world. There had been nothing like it in the past, and it is unlikely that it will ever be seen again. It had at its disposal a total of 650,000 passenger spaces and most of these were filled every day during the operation. On an average day, SCAJAP landed and cleared 25,000 people through Japanese ports. During one record week, they landed and cleared more than 250,000 men, women, and children.

SCAJAP was under the control of Rear Admiral Charles Momsen who held the Navy Cross and Distinguished Service Medal among numerous other decorations. He had achieved considerable fame for organising the rescue in pre-war 1939 of all the crew in the sunken submarine USS *Squalus*. Momsen had also developed the Momsen lung, an emergency escape re-breathing apparatus for submariners. He had spent much of his time as a submariner in World War II sinking Japanese ships and, now here he was, organising ships to bring the Japanese home. At his disposal was the remaining Japanese fleet, consisting of 50 merchantmen and 150 American-built warships, including four aircraft carriers and two cruisers. There were also 105 'liberty ships', including six converted into hospitals. Another 85 landing ship tanks slowly operated throughout the Pacific with thousands of soldiers and civilians and children packed into them. All of these ships were crewed by Japanese seamen and flew the SCAJAP flag, an unusual swallow-tailed green–red configuration unlike any national flag. SCAJAP devised its own flag because the ships were American and could not fly the Japanese flag while the crews were Japanese and could not fly the American flag.

The new Japanese Government wanted to get their people home as soon as possible as much as the host countries wanted to get rid of them. In Indochina and Singapore where the Japanese had been stationed, the Allies were now using Japanese troops as 'police'. In Indonesia after the war had ceased, there were stories circulating that Dutch, Australian and Japanese forces were firing upon Indonesian rebels as a coalition. That such a hated enemy could now be seen as being in charge was an abhorrent idea that encouraged host countries to expedite their return to Japan.

On the Japanese mainland, the American Army operated nine reception centres for Japanese repatriation. Most of these were in central and western Japan, but one was at Uraga, Yokohama, just two hours' drive from Tokyo. This port was famously where Commodore Perry landed in 1853, starting a chain of events that would change history. A number of Japanese commentators and some Westerners noted the irony that this location is where it all began, the West forcing Japan to open up and, in so doing, helping create a militarist monster.

So these ships were sent out to all corners of the wide Pacific and East Asia for their human cargo, bringing the lost peoples of Japan home. These journeys were not pleasure cruises aboard the *Queen Mary*, but SCAJAP organisers did the best they could to provide for the food and health of the passengers. Despite the best medical efforts, cholera was still a huge problem in Asia and the last thing the Occupation Forces needed was an epidemic throughout Japan. Consequently, ships loaded with both soldiers and civilians suspected of carrying disease and, especially cholera, stayed anchored. At one stage a total of 20 of them flew the yellow quarantine flag until the last case of cholera disappeared. Only then were the soldiers unloaded.

When Naka's ship had been cleared at Japan, he disembarked and his landing craft took him to Uraga where he proceeded through the checking system. While under the control of the United States, it was staffed by Japanese. Repatriates were shunted through a maze which was actually a series of picket lines which kept everyone separated so that there could be no mistake in examining each individual. Prisoners dropped their baggage which was sprayed with DDT and then they stripped out of their hated prisoner uniform and underwent a physical examination. They were also liberally dosed with DDT powder and issued with a Japanese uniform. Luggage and bundles were checked through customs to ensure that they did not bring in contraband, especially weapons. While it was efficient, this whole process still took three days. Naka was given a small sum of money from the Japanese Government and a railway ticket, ready to make the trip to a home that could be a bombed-out city, town, or street.

Noble looked at these men, like him, standing and waiting. In the absence of rank, weapons and insignia, they still bore themselves proudly as military men with the indefinable look of soldiers. Noble was struck by their proud presentation. In a few days, they would reach home and melt back into the general civilian population. Sadly for many, there would be little for them to do unless they were a farmer or a mechanic. At that time in 1946, more than 70 per cent of the demobilised soldiers, a total of 3.5 million, were unemployed and the Japanese Government had no resources, ability or program to care for them. Unlike the victors in this conflict, there was no GI Bill of Rights, no bonuses, no land settlement plan, no retraining, and no special employment office. Large sections of the civilian population now treated them with contempt, which represented an extraordinary change in civilian thinking. Many of those who had loudly praised their heroes during victory now despised and hated them in defeat. The ordinary soldier was blamed for the suffering of a war initiated by high-level militarists, although logic dictated that the ordinary soldier was no more to blame than the citizen who was now grieving.

SCAJAP operated from 1 October 1945 to 31 December 1946. In the end, it had repatriated 5,103,300 Japanese to their homeland—a truly remarkable effort. The remaining 1,316,000 were in Russian hands and sadly were unable to be returned under that program. Their homecoming would be years later.

Normally at that time of year in 1946 it would have been the start of the Cherry Blossom viewing (O-Hanami), a festival much cherished by the Japanese people. Few of these trees would have survived the massive fire bombings of March 1945 and it was reported that what blossoms remained were pale and knocked about by the rain. Like so many returning Japanese, Naka faced an uncertain future and sadly nothing more is known of him. He faced a long journey home to the southern island of Kyushu and would be another one of the war-ghosts. His mother had been told back in 1943 that he was dead. She had received the government compensation and likely spent a portion of it on a modest memorial in his hometown. If he had any remaining soldier friends they would have gone to his mother's house with a memorial box containing 'his ashes'. This lie was common practice and in one way it was meant to be a consolation to the family that his spirit had returned to his home, yet it was still a lie promoted by the militarists. Now that he was home there was the natural relief that a mother and family members would experience—to see their son and brother safe—but it would be short-lived. He and others faced potential ostracism because of his prisoner of war status.

Did he simply blend back into the disjointed amnesiac society that was Japan in 1946? Did he find his family, forgiveness and love—the peace of mind that he so longed for and yet could never achieve? He was a product of his time, upbringing, personality and society. His life was ultimately shaped by circumstances beyond his control, like the small boat tossed on the tempest in the classical Japanese woodcut, 'The Great Wave'. He also struggled with what it is to be an individual bound by ties of honour and duty, fear and failure.

EPILOGUE

A JUDGEMENT

In the end, was Maseo Naka the crucial and critical bellwether, inspiration and motivator for the devastating breakout at Cowra in August 1944?

While it has been claimed, with a touch of 1940s racial stereotyping, 'that if one Japanese was known, all Japanese are known', the experience of the Allies during World War II told a different story. The Japanese soldier fighting in the field became a different person after capture. Once imprisoned, the feared militancy, fanaticism, and obstinacy mostly melted away under humane, decent treatment and good handling by the Allies. In captivity they gradually realised an important truth that almost all they had been told about the Western Allies, including their conduct towards prisoners, was false. In essence, the insights and understanding of those early prisoners was two to three years ahead of those who surrendered after the emperor's edict in 1945. Soldiers still fighting and who were ordered by their emperor on 15 August to lay down their arms would only know the truth about Japan's war after they had returned to a wrecked and wasted homeland. There they would also find another surprising reality, that of how forgiving and generous the victorious Allies would be.

In examining Naka's role in the Cowra breakout, one should also remember the historical political conflicts within the imperial armed forces. The Japanese Navy and Army had been intolerant rivals since their establishment in the 19th century. Prior to World War II in 1936, there had even been an uprising of young commissioned army officers, who saw themselves as representing the 'pure' Japanese. These 'Young Turks' rebelled against what they saw as 'the corrupt and un-Japanese' government in Tokyo. At the time, the army officers were viewed as the conservative traditionalists while the navy officers were more moderate. Later in 1941 it was the navy, which had to be convinced to participate in the attack on Pearl Harbor. This 'moderates versus traditionalists' rivalry that was ever present in Japan before the war had resurfaced in Cowra, but in a surprising way.

When the navy and army men were mingled together in B Compound at Cowra, the reverse dynamic occurred. On a numbers basis, while most prisoners were from the army, they represented the moderates. The traditionalist or more hardline elements were from the navy. This strange situation was probably due to the time of capture of the different groups and their diverging conditions before their surrender. Simply put, most of the navy prisoners had been captured early in the war when Japan had still been able to keep transport routes open for adequate supplies. They had also served in the relative comfort of modern, capable warships with full rations. For them, the war was still being won and was eminently winnable. The majority of the army prisoners, on the other hand, had endured and suffered to breaking point in life-and-death campaigns. These desperate battles in New Guinea and New Britain had also been accompanied by chronic lack of rations leading, in some cases, to the ultimate savagery, cannibalism. Not only had they fought and lost, but they had been defeated decisively. These soldiers had seen the incredible resources, firepower and resolve of the Allies who were intent on taking this fight all the way back to their home islands.

B Compound at Cowra therefore became a metaphor for the Japanese Imperial forces as a whole—a battle-weary, realistic army group versus the stubborn fighting spirit of the navy men. This situation was compounded by the ordinary Japanese prisoner's lack of understanding about his status under the Geneva Convention. While Japan had not been a signatory to this agreement, which provided a number of important rights to prisoners of war, Australia was, and even treated Japanese prisoners of war over and above the standard required by the Convention. Not only had Japan not signed but it had never instructed its soldiers about their status and rights if they were captured by a country that was a signatory. This disconnect between their actual rights and status and the lack of this advice, allowed the hardliners to enforce the iron battlefield instruction of

'Never dishonour yourself by being captured while you are alive.' To a great extent, this forced Japanese soldiers, sailors and pilots to live their life in fear of the shame of ever being a prisoner. Similarly they also believed they would be executed by the Allies so either way they would die! While the proportion of army to navy men was 80:20 in B Compound, it was the navy officers who exerted their will through intimidation and, as a result, dominated. This was the same ratio, interestingly, who supposedly determined that the breakout should go ahead. This coincidence casts some doubt on this so-called ballot result.

Recent research has provided a new understanding of the sequence of events that led to the breakout. This analysis has arisen from older Japanese ex-prisoners of war now speaking frankly about what actually happened. Gleaned from survivors who were prepared to express these views much later in life, the evidence is far from anecdotal. Masaru Moriki from Naka's unit, for instance, said that he and his friend had actually baked a cake in readiness to celebrate the move to Hay. Many other regular soldiers were said to be pleased to get away from the regular intimidation they experienced from their NCOs (non-commissioned officers). This new information is revealing because it is from the men who experienced this situation firsthand with no apparent motive for embellishment. What gives their testimony special weight is that it would have been far easier for them to speak of the 'united will' of B Compound to rise up and break out rather than betray their comrades many years later by highlighting division.

On the direct cause of the breakout, it now seems clear that the decision to move all prisoners of war below the rank of lance-corporal to the Hay camp was lacking in sense, logic and judgement from a number of perspectives. Those charged with the responsibility of running the various prison camps where the Japanese were held during the war generally operated on the principle of 'security only' with only a general understanding of the impact of their decisions on their captives. There is little evidence at Cowra that the camp's intelligence section had any real influence on the day-to-day security of the Japanese. This was in spite of the skill and talent of its officers, their best efforts and the vital role that intelligence should have played in such decisions.

It seems, oddly enough, that there was actually more interest in the Italians and in keeping the fractious royalist and fascist elements apart. As part of their management of the fascist prisoners, overly influential or disruptive individuals were regularly moved around and constantly monitored to reduce their influence. They were also subject to lengthy interviews, with a number of informants only too happy to enlighten the authorities on perceived 'enemies' from within. Despite the far greater threat they posed, there is little evidence that the Cowra staff used similar techniques on the Japanese. Had they done so, they may well have been able to identify and separate the hardliners from the more compliant and relaxed Japanese prisoners. It seems that the approach was a basic one, in that Japanese prisoners of war were to be simply locked up.

The Australians must have known that separating a large group of Japanese soldiers with the rank of private, without the control and discipline provided by non-commissioned officers and commissioned officers, would be a recipe for trouble. While the numbers in B Compound at Cowra were escalating to dangerous levels, there is every reason to believe that a meeting with the Japanese leaders would have been successful in addressing the overcrowding problem. While consulting enemy prisoners on issues of security may not have been palatable, it was an accepted method of keeping the peace and 'lowering the tone' in prison camps. The evidence also shows from the conversations between the Australian (Ramsay) and the Japanese leaders (Kanazawa, Kojima, Yamakawa and Minami) on the day before the breakout, that this may well have been the case. The demeanour of the four Japanese and their apparent willingness to negotiate over the transfers indicates that the leaders were receptive to compromise. When that was refused point-blank, with the devastating loss of face that this rebuttal entailed, their hands were effectively forced. The decision of the Cowra authorities to unilaterally transfer the prisoners was, at best, lacking in judgement. The reasoning was doubly flawed when one considers what was already known from earlier prisoners and particularly from Maseo Naka. He encapsulated the extreme example of a Japanese captive; however, the Australians seemed to model their controls, systems and security measures on the moderate and passive prisoners. The official reports and observations by many Allied staff, of Naka's single-minded efforts to atone for his dishonour because of the loss of his family of soldiers from his platoon, should have contributed significantly to this understanding.

* * *

Over many years I attempted, with the help of other researchers, to find out what happened to Naka-san. He was born in 1919 so it is possible, allowing for the extreme old age reached by many Japanese, that he is still alive. Tracking down Japanese ex-military personnel from World War II is extremely difficult, unless they want to be found and then make themselves available. Even in postwar Japan, being a prisoner of war carried a heavy stigma. Being taken a prisoner in the field of battle placed a Japanese soldier in a completely different category from those who surrendered in August 1945, after being ordered to do so by their emperor. Japanese prisoners still carried a dishonour and, in most cases, hid their shame from friends and family. Some did not care but the majority of ex-prisoners of war simply stayed quiet. When some wives found out that their husbands (who they had married after the war) had been prisoners, they declared that, had they known, they would not have wed.

Through the courtesy of Mayor Bill West from Cowra, I contacted the Japanese Embassy in Canberra about the fate of Maseo Naka, but to no avail. I was advised politely that Japanese privacy laws forbid any contact or other information being passed on to people other than relatives. Letters to the Japanese Social Welfare and War Victims' Relief Bureau, Ministry of Health, Labour and Welfare requesting a search for Naka's records went unanswered. I contacted the successors of his original employer MBK in Kyushu who happily undertook thorough checks of their personnel records, also with no luck. Marist priest and former missionary in Japan, Paul Glynn, even had a friend visit the modern equivalent of Naka's pre-war address in Kyushu but again with no luck. There was even an inquiry as to whether his address may have actually been in Hiroshima, but contacts through the city authorities brought no results. I am quite certain that Naka's original records exist as they were returned by the United States to Japan in the 1950s. These records are, unfortunately, not indexed and one needs to be either a relative or have the permission of a relative to locate, read and consult these. Humorously, the strict nature of Japan's privacy laws can lead to quite unusual and unexpected consequences. As one government department may not be allowed to know what information another department has, there is anecdotal evidence that pensions have been paid to families whose parents have been dead for years! One wonders if it would take a number of *Ojiisan* (grandfathers) to turn 100 plus to make the payments stop! It is genuinely hoped that in the near future the Japanese Government will join the rest of the world and open its records to researchers.

I have lived in Cowra for nearly 30 years and in that time have met dozens of Australians and Japanese who were at the camp at Cowra as guards and prisoners. At the time of writing only two or three ex-prisoners are still alive with a similarly small number of Australians. Even up to the early 2000s, a number of Japanese prisoners returned to visit what they called the: 'University of Cowra where they learned about life'. One of the last, Teruo Murakami (mentioned earlier), returned for the 70th Anniversary of the Cowra Breakout. Years before another ex-prisoner told me he was so grateful to the Australian soldiers who in combat had shot him multiple times with an Owen gun. Had he not been shot, then captured and treated, he said, he would have surely died of starvation in the New Guinea jungle. Many of these men were so affected and imbued by their time at Cowra and the spirit of survival, they subsequently formed organisations back in Japan after their return such as 'Kochi New Guinea' and 'Cowra Kai', where, as ex-prisoners of war they could meet in comradeship and friendship. These men were not ashamed of their history, with Cowra Kai even producing an anniversary book with the names and photographs of their members. One even built a set of housing units and named them 'Cowra'.

EPILOGUE

In researching and writing this book, I have not intended to be combative or intentionally provocative but rather to set out my experiences while investigating Naka's story. My admiration for modern-day Japan is almost boundless and my wife and I truly like the place and enjoy the company of our Japanese friends who feel similarly attracted to Australia and to Cowra. For the Westerner, there are many qualities in the Japanese people that are familiar, but Japan is, nevertheless, enigmatic, and parts of it will, I suspect, forever remain mysterious to the outside world. As far as the past is concerned, anglophile Australians in the 1940s certainly had their prejudices; however, I suspect that those who were in contact with Naka had a level of admiration for him, even if it was solely on the basis of it being soldier to soldier.

* * *

In the end, Maseo Naka was just one man, but his fanatical sense of honour and duty embodied what most Australians at the time thought about the Japanese. Now at a time many years after World War II we can take a more objective and balanced view of him. In 1983, Lieutenant Colonel Ralph Honner, the exceptional leader of the 39th Battalion in New Guinea, addressed a meeting of Japanese Kochi New Guinea ex-servicemen in Melbourne.[32] In the plainest language, Honner said that there may have been a natural hesitation about former hated enemies meeting in such a situation. He went on to say that both sides could now recognise that they experienced war and, through it, they could now contribute to building the peace. He pointed out that the Australians remembered their comrades and how they still supported each other, even those who were injured or had passed away. The Australians also remembered, he added, the enemy's hardships and their courage. They admired their battle tactics and military spirit and concluded: 'We can imagine that your comradeship or human natures were the same as we Australians.' On that occasion, these sentiments were reciprocated by the group leader

32 Recorded in *Cowra Uprising—One Survivor's Memoir* (Masaru Moriki, 1983), translated by Midori Treeve.

of Kochi New Guinea, Masaru Moriki, who was from Maseo Naka's regiment which had fought the Australians in New Guinea. Overall, it was a most agreeable meeting with old enemies sitting down with each other and swapping tales, with sign language and mud maps drawn on pieces of paper making up for the language differences. Moriki subsequently visited Cowra on a number of occasions and played a prominent part in the commemorations of the 50th Anniversary of the Cowra Breakout in 1994. A large photograph of him with Australian guard Wal Mackenzie hangs on the wall at Cowra Visitor Information Centre with the title 'Old foes … now old friends.'

Hopefully, in the end, Maseo Naka had a long and relatively happy life in the new, progressive, outward-looking Japan. Stranger things have happened!

ACKNOWLEDGEMENTS

Maseo Naka's name is recorded in various forms being Maseo, Masao and Masso. I have settled on Maseo.

- Professor Peter Stanley, University of New South Wales, Canberra, at the Australian Defence Force Academy for his wisdom and guidance.
- David Dixon for editing services.
- The Australian War Memorial for permission to use images from their collections.
- Harumi Sakaguchi for his advice, particularly on matters relating to Japanese prisoners of war and their families.
- Alister Kentwell for sharing his time during World War II as an interrogator with the Allied Translator and Interpreter Section.
- Captain Dennis Magennis, Museum of Army Intelligence, Canungra, Queensland and The Hon Angus Taylor MP and The Hon Kevin Andrews MP for their assistance in research on the mysterious 'Miss James'.
- Cowra Shire Council for permission to use photographs and documents in their collection.
- Gordon Rolls, President of the Cowra Breakout Association and son of Private Alfred Rolls; and Harvey Nicholson, Vice President of the Cowra Breakout Association.
- Dr Richard White, Fellow of the Royal Australian and New Zealand College of Psychiatrists and a Member of the Royal College of Psychiatrists (UK) for his advice on mental health treatments and observations on Naka's situation.
- Lawrance Ryan of Cowra for his constant encouragement, assistance and permission to use images.
- Greg McNally SC for his assistance with interviews with Justice John Slattery, AO, QC, KCSG.

- Father Paul Glynn SM for his advice and guidance over the years.
- The late Harry Gordon, CMG, AM for his advice and his research into the Cowra Breakout.
- Dr Keiko Tamura and Dr Steven Bullard from the Australian War Memorial Australia–Japan Research project for their advice and assistance.
- The staff of the National Archives of Australia who care for our nation's treasure of historical records.
- The Nagakura Foundation for their research and attempts to locate Maseo Naka.
- Dr Anita Heiss for her particular perspectives on Cowra and the breakout.
- My wife Ann, for her constant encouragement, support and suggestions.
- Michelle York, Gunnedah, NSW, for cover design.
- Lieutenant-Colonel Neil Smith for research on the 55/53 Battalion.
- Actor Yutaka Izumihara for permission to use his image on the front cover.

SOURCES

- Asada, T, *The Night of a Thousand Suicides*, translated from Japanese by Ray Cowan, previously published in 1967, Angus & Robertson, North Ryde, NSW, 1985.
- Boorman, L, *Pickhandle Parade—Memoirs of the Cowra Breakout*, 1998.
- Bullard, S, *Japanese Army Operations in the South Pacific Area. New Britain and Papua Campaigns 1942–43*, Australia-Japan Research Project, Australian War Memorial, 2007.
- Bullard, S and Tamura, K (eds), *From a Hostile Shore—Australia and Japan at war in New Guinea*, Australia–Japan Research Project, Australian War Memorial, 2004.
- Carr-Gregg, M, *Japanese Prisoners of War in Revolt: The Outbreaks at Featherston and Cowra during World War 2*, University of Queensland Press, St Lucia, Qld, 1978.
- Charleton, P, *War Against Japan 1941–1942*, Time Life, North Sydney, 1988.
- Clarke, H, *Escape to Death*, Random House Australia, Sydney, 1965.
- Collie, C and Marutani, H, *The Path of Infinite Sorrow*, Allen & Unwin, Crows Nest, Australia, 2009.
- Cook, HT and Cook, TF, *Japan at War an Oral History*, The New Press, New York, 1992.
- Daugherty III, LJ, *Fighting Techniques of a Japanese Infantryman 1941–1945,* MBI Publishing, USA, 2002.
- Dower, John W, *War Without Mercy—Race & Power in the Pacific War*, Pantheon Books, New York, 1993.
- Gibney, F (ed), *Sensoo—The Japanese Remember the Pacific War*, An East Gate Book, ME Sharpe, New York and London, 2007.

- Gordon, H, *Die Like the Carp!*, Cassell Australia, Stanmore, 1978.
- Gordon, H, *Voyage from Shame*, UQP Australia, Brisbane, 1994.
- Ham, P, *Kokoda*, Harper Collins, Australia, 2004.
- Harries, Meirion, *Soldiers of the Sun—The Rise and Fall of the Imperial Japanese Army*, Random House, New York, 1991.
- Harrison, H, *The Brave Japanese*, Rigby Limited, Adelaide, 1966.
- Hastings, M, *Nemesis: The Battle for Japan 1944–45*, Harper Press, London, 2007.
- Havens, TRH, *Valley of Darkness: The Japanese People and World War Two*, University Press of America, London, 1978.
- Henderson, James, *Onward, Boy Soldiers: The Battle for Milne Bay*, Nedlands, Western Australia: University of Western Australia, 1992.
- Ienaga Saburoo, *The Pacific War 1931–1945*, Pantheon Books, New York, 1968.
- Lord Russell of Liverpool CBE, MC, *The Knights of Bushido: A short history of Japanese war crimes*, Corgi Books, 1958.
- Mackenzie, Kenneth Seaforth, *Dead Men Rising*, A&R Classics, 1951.
- Milner, S, *United States Army in World War II—The War in the Pacific—Victory in Papua*, Office of the Chief of Military History Department of the Army, Washington, DC, 1957.
- Nakano, Fujio, 'Cowra Revisited' (1983) *Geo: Australasia's Geographical Magazine* 5, 102–11.
- Nitobe, Inazo, *Bushido—the Soul of Japan*, Teibi Publishing Company, 1899.
- Moriki, M, *Cowra Uprising: One Survivor's Memoir*, Translated from Japanese by Midoori Treeve, GD & M Treeve, Wodonga, Vic., 1998.
- Page, A, *Between Victor and Vanquished: an Australian Interrogator in the War against Japan*, Australian Military History, Loftus, NSW, 2008.
- Potts, ED and Potts, A, *Yanks Down Under, 1941–45: The American Impact on Australia*, London, Oxford University Press, 1985.

- Rottman, GL, *Japanese Army in World War II—The South Pacific and New Guinea, 1942–43*, Osprey Publishing, Oxford, 2005.
- Straus, U, *The Anguish of Surrender—Japanese POWs of World War II*, University of Washington Press, Seattle and London, 2003.
- Taya Cook, H, and Cook, TF, *Japan at War—an Oral History*, The New Press, New York, London, 1992.
- Toland, John, *The Rising Sun—The Decline and Fall of the Japanese Empire, 1936–1945*, The Modern Library, New York, 2003.
- White, O, *Green Armour*, Angus and Robertson, Sydney and London, 1945.

Official Histories

- Dexter, DS, *Australia in the War of 1939–1945*, Series 1 Army Volumes VI, Canberra Australian War Memorial, Griffin Press, Adelaide, 1957.
- McCarthy, D, *Australia in the War of 1939–1945*, Series 1 Army Volumes V, Canberra Australian War Memorial, Griffin Press, Adelaide, 1957.
- Wigmore, L, *Australia in the War of 1939–1945*, Series 1 Army Volumes IV, Canberra Australian War Memorial, Griffin Press, Adelaide, 1957.

US Military documents and publications

- Milner S, *Victory in Papua The War in the Pacific, United States Army in World War II*, Centre of Military History, United States Army, Washington DC, 1989.
- United States War Department, *Soldier's Guide to the Japanese Army*, Special series No. 27, 15 November 1944, United States Government Printing Office, Washington, 1944.
- United States War Department, *Jungle Warfare, War Department Field Manual*, FM 72-20, United States Government Printing Office, Washington, 1944.

Archival sources

National Archives of Australia

- Cowra NSW—Compulsory Acquisition of Defence Land for Site for Prisoner of War Camp 18 June Series number A60741942—Claim of the State of New South Wales Control symbol PO5011 Contents date range 1942–1942.
- Cowra POW [Prisoner of War] camp acquisition [Box No 538] Series number SP857/3 Control symbol CL/10187 Contents date range 1942–1951.
- Cowra POW camp—selection of site [1.0cm; box 21] Series number SP1008/1 Control symbol 420/34/19 Contents date range 1941–1941.
- Directorate of Prisoners of War [POW or prisoners of war] and Internees—1939–1951—Volumes 1 and 2, National Archives of Australia Series Number A7711.
- Military Court—PWJ (USA) Lieutenant NAKA, Masso [Box 170] Series number SP459/1 Control symbol 489/3/1313 Contents date range 1943–1943, National Archives of Australia.
- Prisoner of War/Internee: Yamashita aka Naka, Hideo Masao Maseo; Date of birth—22 February 1919; Nationality—Japanese Series number MP1103/1 Series accession number MP1103/1/0 National Archives of Australia.
- Prisoner of War/Internee; Naka, Maseo; Year of birth—1919; Nationality—Japanese Series number MP1103/2 Control symbol prisoners of war JA145359 Contents date range 1939–1945 National Archives of Australia.

Australian War Memorial

- Interrogation File Masao Naka.
- AWM 61 S56/2/832 Establishment of Mulyan Prisoner of War Camp Farm Cowra.

Other

- New South Wales Department of Health—Records on Masao Naka and Shichijo Shojiro.

Personal letters and documents and notes

- Letter from Alan Jackson to Prisoner of War Camp Working Party on recollections of his time at Cowra, 3 August 1993.
- Letter from Duncan F Chapman to Prisoner of War Camp Working Party on recollections of his time at Cowra, 14 April 1991.
- Notes on author's conversation with Jim Baillie from Canberra, orderly at the Cowra Camp Hospital, 2006.
- Notes from author's conversation with Lionel Boorman, Warrant Officer II at Intelligence Section Cowra Camp, 21 November 1978.